Dept of English,
University of Port Elizabeth,
1991

COMMUNICAMUS 7

Theoretical approaches to communication

COMMUNICAMUS

Presented by the Department of Communication of the University of South Africa

Titles that have appeared in the COMMUNICAMUS series:

THEORETICAL APPROACHES TO COMMUNICATION

NERINA JANSEN
SHEILA STEINBERG

JUTA & CO, LTD
1991

First Edition 1991

© Juta & Co Ltd, 1991

P.O. Box 14373, Kenwyn 7790

ISBN 0 7021 2488 5

Set in 10 on 12 pt Melior, printed on 74 g/m^2 Oyster Opaque and bound in the Republic of South Africa by Creda Press, Solan Road, Cape Town

Contents

Foreword

Although most communicologists, at least occasionally, refer to "theory", this concept is frequently misconstrued and its significance in scientific practice underestimated. Terminological confusion among theorists themselves contributes to the largely negative view of theory. Small wonder then that very few authors have hitherto attempted the difficult task of defining "theory" and determining its role in scientific practice.

This monograph is a modest attempt to clarify some of the misunderstanding concerning theory and to introduce the reader to the fascinating field of general communication theory. Due to lack of space it is only an *introduction* to the field.

The first chapter examines the concept of theory and suggests that it consists of several parts, while various levels of theorising may be distinguished in scientific practice. Following from the viewpoint that theory, in the final analysis, is a body of theoretical approaches, the field of general communication theory is divided into two main groups, namely approaches concerning the phenomenon of communication as such and approaches concerning the assessment of its quality. Both categories are subdivided in turn.

The body of the monograph consists of a discussion of theoretical approaches and theories deriving from them. To highlight how multi-faceted the phenomenon of communication is, and to emphasise how limited any individual approach or theory must be, as many approaches and theories as possible have been included.

In Chapters 2 to 6 the introduction delimits the approach and the representative theories discussed, then the chosen theories are explained and critically assessed in the remainder of the chapter. A short résumé, which stresses the need for an adequate understanding of theory and a continuous critical appraisal of theoretical approaches, concludes the monograph.

Although the authors did not take an equal share in writing the monograph, they jointly accept responsibility for its contents and shortcomings.

Nerina Jansen
Sheila Steinberg
Pretoria
January 1991

Chapter 1

The concept of theory

1.1 INTRODUCTION

Although communicologists generally recognise the need for theory, it is frequently argued that "too much theory" leads to armchair philosophising which divorces scientific investigation from the "real facts" about communication. The growing popularity of and public demand for "facts" derived from quantitative scientific research even raises, for some people, the question as to whether society can afford the luxury of theorising. This profound misunderstanding of the nature and significance of theory in scientific practice focuses the researcher and practitioner's attention on the requirements for empirical study and the need for refining study methods, while the conceptualisation of problems, for example, is relegated to a secondary position.

However, misunderstanding concerning the meaning and significance of theory in scientific endeavour arises from terminological confusion as well. Even theorists themselves are frequently guilty of imprecise and ambiguous definition and arbitrary usage of terms. Some theorists are even uncertain about the nature of their own activities! It is therefore not strange that they try to "simplify" theory by offering practical illustrations of what it can tell us about communication. Communication models, which are so popular in American textbooks, are a case in point. Such attempts often add to existing confusion, because they reveal an underlying misunderstanding concerning the premises on which scientific reasoning ultimately rests.

This chapter sets out to clarify some crucial issues concerning theory. While it certainly does not claim to offer final answers, it suggests a useful way for determining the meaning of the concept

1

of theory and the role of theory in scientific practice. It is shown that some concepts generally used in conjunction with theory in fact describe different components of theory or levels of theorising. The comprehensive definition of the concept of theory which is formulated on the basis of the discussion, serves to highlight the indispensable role of theorising in scientific practice.

1.2 THEORY AND THEORISING

Scientific practice involves a deliberately planned and disciplined search for knowledge concerning the phenomenon of communication. Each investigator delimits his/her study of the phenomenon by conceptualising a "problem" for investigation. What constitutes a problem, in turn, depends on the investigator's theoretical approach, that is, his/her way of looking at the phenomenon of communication. While the conceptualisation of the problem precedes the actual empirical research, the view of communication from which the conceptualisation is derived guides the entire process of investigation.

The multi-faceted nature of communication precludes the possibility of a complete or final view of it. Each theoretical approach inevitably offers a limited view which highlights only certain aspects of the phenomenon. Characteristic of the history of social scientific practice is a continuous controversy about the suitability of different theoretical approaches to communication, a phenomenon that stimulates, rather than retards, the growth of scientific disciplines. The controversy in communication studies accentuates the need for an ongoing and never-ending process of investigation in which the phenomenon of communication is constantly approached from different viewpoints and examined through the conceptualisation of new problems.

Theory is basically a body of theoretical approaches to communication. Thus, to understand the nature of theory and to be able to fully appreciate its role in scientific practice, one must examine the nature of the theoretical approach.

1.2.1 The theoretical approach

Since the nature of the theoretical approach is revealed in its structure, this section examines the constituent parts of the structure and their interrelationships. The components of the theoretical approach involve different levels of generality, the assumptions being the most general and the concepts the most specific level within the approach.

1.2.1.1 Underlying assumptions

Different theoretical approaches view the phenomenon of communication differently because they have different assumptions concerning its nature and human participants. *Ontological* assumptions describe the nature and composition of the phenomenon, that is, its characteristics, constituent parts and their mutual relationships, while *anthropological* assumptions define the nature of human participation in communication and the nature of the relationships between communicating human beings. The two categories of assumptions are intertwined and mutually dependent on each other.

Ontological and anthropological assumptions are accompanied by *epistemological* assumptions which define the nature of knowledge and prescribe the way in which it may be gained. Since the latter assumptions are more closely associated with the actual investigation they are only mentioned in passing in this monograph.

The most important consequence of the ontological and anthropological assumptions of a theoretical approach is that they determine what may be investigated by the approach in question. By offering a description of the phenomenon of communication and showing how human beings are involved in it, the assumptions of a theoretical approach pinpoint those aspects that are, for the purposes of the approach, fundamental to an understanding of communication. Specific problems are only conceptualised within the range of relevant aspects thus delimited, while other aspects concerning the phenomenon are disregarded.

Since any theoretical approach inevitably offers a limited view of communication, the need for considering the suitability of available approaches before embarking on a specific study can hardly be overemphasised. This is all the more important since exponents of theoretical approaches tend to assume that their views capture the very essence of communication, while other approaches are incapable of doing so. In this sense theoretical approaches are inherently ideological, whether or not their followers explicitly acknowledge their view of a desirable state of affairs.

The assumptions of a theoretical approach are embodied in different theories. Individual theories, of which several are found in any scientific discipline, constitute the second component of the theoretical approach.

1.2.1.2 Theories

Authors frequently confuse theory (a body of theoretical approaches) with *a* theory. Since the same view of communication may be expressed in different ways, any theoretical approach generates a number of individual theories, each of which represents a particular version of the same view. To appreciate the existence of different theories within the same approach, it is useful to examine some of the ways in which they may differ from one another.

Two obvious differences between individual theories concern their focus and scope. Although theories within the same approach share the same view of communication, each selects for investigation only some of the relevant aspects delimited by the approach which they represent. Depending on the number of aspects highlighted, individual theories may be more or less comprehensive in scope.

An important difference between individual theories concerns their level of generality. Some theories, for instance, offer a view that may apply to the entire phenomenon and thus to (nearly) all empirical examples of communication, while other theories only apply to some or even to one specific aspect and/or example of communication. The first-mentioned theories were particularly popular in the early history of communication studies. A classic example is Walter Lipmann's theory of public opinion. Some of these "grand theories" are in fact so general and comprehensive that they may be regarded as theoretical approaches rather than theories. For this reason it is often claimed that they do not easily lend themselves to empirical testing.

Theories dealing with a specific aspect(s) and/or example or category of examples of communication are said to be "verifiable". Investigators usually have this kind of theory in mind when they use the term "theory". Although there is considerable variation, verifiable theories generally provide a plausible description or explanation of the way in which variable factors or conditions operate or interrelate in a given case. The "theory" is tested in empirical research by "comparing" it with real life examples of communication in which the said conditions obtain. The results of empirical research, whether or not they confirm the theory, constitute "scientific knowledge" and thus form part of the body of knowledge gained during communicological investigation.

While the need for individual verifiable theories is not denied, it must be emphasised that the value of a one-sided accentuation of "verifiable theory" is dubious, if not outright meaningless. Even the most limited verifiable theory implies a particular view of communication and, unless the investigator is familiar with this view, he/she will fail to promote scientific understanding of communication. After all, what can results tell us about communication if we do not know what we mean by communication and to what the results actually apply?

An important way in which individual theories differ is their terminology. Since each theory only deals with certain aspects delimited by the assumptions of the theoretical approach which they represent, individual theories develop a distinctive terminology to address their chosen aspects. However, the same terms may well occur in more than one theory. The decisive matter in this case is the meaning attached to the common terms, that is, the *concepts* used by different theories.

A theory basically consists of a number of interrelated concepts. Hence the concept is the third component of the theoretical approach.

1.2.1.3 Concepts

Concepts are simply words to which we attach specific meanings. Like the concepts of everyday speech, scientific concepts denote and define aspects of the phenomenon of communication. By thus imposing a structure on the phenomenon, concepts reduce the variability of real life examples of communication and identify some characteristics which enable us to get a grip on the phenomenon.

In order to converse meaningfully, communicologists must know the meanings of concepts and consistently use them "correctly". Terminological confusion and indiscriminate use of concepts clouds understanding of their meaning and divorces concepts from the context in which they are meant to appear. Concepts are only meaningful in relation to other concepts with which they combine to form a theory. While the assumptions of the theoretical approach pinpoint the relevant aspects for conceptualisation and investigation, the theories which emanate from the approach provide concepts to define these aspects and show how the concepts should be related to one another.

The dynamic and ever-changing nature of the phenomenon of communication precludes the possibility of universally valid concepts and theories. Constant revision of existing concepts and theories, and the creation of new ones to capture the changing nature of communication, is therefore a prerequisite for scientific practice.

The theoretical approach is the highest level of theorising on which most theorists encounter theory. However, to offer a more complete picture, two more general levels of theorising are briefly mentioned.

1.2.2 Paradigms and metatheory

The term "paradigm" is used in a number of ways and for different purposes. To show its significance in scientific practice only one of its meanings is discussed.

"Paradigm" refers to a central idea or viewpoint shared by a number of theoretical approaches. Depending on the idea used as criterion, several paradigms may be formulated and the same theoretical approach may appear in more than one of them. In the social sciences the so-called "deterministic" paradigm is a well-known example. The central idea is that the human being's life is largely shaped by (social) forces beyond his/her control and that such forces determine the nature and meaning of communication as well. Diverse theoretical approaches, such as functionalism (see Chapter 2, Section 2.2), general system theory (see Chapter 3, Section 3.3) and varieties of neo-Marxism (see Chapter 5) subscribe to this notion.

The central notion suggested by a paradigm may shape scientific thinking for a long time. This idea is often considered as an answer to a crucial problem posed by a particular discipline. As long as the paradigm remains unchallenged by competing paradigms, theoretical approaches tend to support its view and to differ merely in the ways in which they express it.

The central idea of a paradigm may also be used to describe the nature and borderlines of a field of study, such as Communication. Compare, for example, the "transfer of information" paradigm with the "constitution of meaning" paradigm. In each case the paradigm offers a description of the nature of communication and maintains that all investigation must consider matters relating to the nature of the phenomenon as described by the paradigm. In this sense several contrasting paradigms may be found in any scientific discipline at a given time and each paradigm may be represented by different theoretical approaches. The "constitution of meaning" paradigm, for example, is represented by theoretical approaches such as existentialism, symbolic interactionism, phenomenology and semiology. While all of them emphasise the centrality of meaning in the study of communication, each offers its own distinctive view of aspects such as the nature of meaning, the process whereby it is constituted and the significance of meaning for the phenomenon of communication (see Chapter 4).

An even higher, or more general, level of theorising is that of *metatheory*. In this case we deal with theory and theorising about theory. Topics such as the nature of theory and theorising and criteria for determining the suitability of scientific explanations are relevant to metatheory. In fact, metatheory deals with the process of conceptualisation and theory-building as such. In Communication very little has been done on this level of theorising.

1.2.3 Taxonomies and models

The concepts of taxonomy and model are often used in conjunction with theory. To be able to appreciate their significance in theorising their meaning is briefly explained.

A *taxonomy* is a list of concepts that denotes aspects of the phenomenon of communication which may be investigated. Taxonomies do not relate to any particular theoretical approach; hence they do not reveal or suggest a particular view of communication. Since relationships between concepts are not explicitly or deliberately indicated, taxonomies do not constitute theories either.

Theorising does not necessarily involve the use of taxonomies and they are by no means indispensable tools for theorising. But, by pointing out what aspects of a phenomenon are or may be important for study purposes, taxonomies are particularly useful for "mapping" a new field of study.

Communication *models* offer a representation of the phenomenon of communication by accentuating certain parts of it and showing the (mutual) relationships between them. The parts that are accentuated are regarded as the most important parts of the phenomenon for the purposes of the model, or even for the study of communication as such. The representation of communication offered by a model is generally expressed diagrammatically or graphically, while verbal and/or mathematical symbols convey the relevant information.

Communication models originated in the early days of American communication studies and well-known examples include the models of Shannon and Weaver, Barnlund, Lasswell, Westley and Maclean and Schramm. Models were particularly popular from the late 1940s to the early 1960s, but American and European examples still appear today. The interested reader may consult McQuail and Windahl (1981) for an overview of mass communication models.

Given their simplified version of communication, models accompany theories, rather than theoretical approaches, and may be used to present a "summary" of a theory. It is interesting to note that such theories almost exclusively follow from positivist approaches, such as functionalism and general system theory. Approaches which describe communication as an ever-evolving process, for example a process in which the constitution of meaning is of crucial significance, do not usually generate models, a fact which illustrates one of the most important shortcomings of models. Models tend to present a static view of communication and, even if they try to show that a dynamic process is involved, they fail to capture its essence and ever-changing character.

Generally speaking, models may be useful for organising and classifying research findings, showing gaps in existing knowledge and generating research about specific aspects of communication. Given their visual impact, models impress persons who seek practical illustrations of what communication looks like, how it works, where problems may occur and how they may be solved. But, since they only highlight certain aspects of a complex process and offer a simplistic representation of the aspects covered, models inevitably distort reality. In addition, it should be noted that the aspects accentuated by a model are deliberately chosen to serve a particular purpose and that the choice of aspects may reflect bias on the part of the investigator. This possibility highlights the need for careful consideration of the purpose of a particular model and for applying a model only for the purpose it is meant to serve.

Finally, it should be noted that, despite the usefulness of models, they are not indispensable parts of theory or theorising.

1.2.4 The significance of theory in scientific practice

Theory is indispensable to scientific practice. Not only is theory the starting-point for scientific investigation, it steers the entire process of investigation and, finally, constitutes the body of scientific findings about communication.

First, by conceptualising the phenomenon of communication, or an aspect of it, theory acts as the starting-point in any investigation. Since no one is capable of viewing a complex phenomenon all at once, communicologists approach and conceptualise communication from different viewpoints. In this sense theory is a body of theoretical approaches. Starting from its own distinctive view of communication, each theoretical approach highlights certain aspects of the phenomenon and focuses the investigator's attention on these, rather than other, aspects. A research project is specifically designed to investigate some of the aspects thus delimited. Seen as a whole, theory defines the subject matter of the discipline of Communication.

Second, by providing assumptions that define the premises on which the investigation rests, theory guides the entire process of scientific investigation. While ontological and anthropological assumptions define those aspects of communication that may be regarded as suitable topics for investigation, epistemological assumptions determine what is regarded as "knowledge" about communication and in what ways it may be gained. Thus the assumptions of theoretical approaches determine not only the subject matter for investigation, but the criteria for conducting "scientific" investigation of the subject matter. Methodological considerations concerning the way in which an investigation will be conducted derive from epistemological considerations.

Finally, by providing a context for interpreting the results, theory substantiates scientific investigation. By thus attributing meaning to the findings, theory organises the knowledge gained in such a way that it may contribute to an understanding of the phenomenon of communication and may stimulate a further search for knowledge. Since the search for knowledge derives from, and is substantiated by theory, this term in fact denotes the totality of scientific reasoning about the phenomenon of communication (Jansen 1990: 16). In this sense the scientific discipline of Communication is defined by its theory. Stated differently, theory is the very substance of a discipline, such as Communication.

Lack of understanding of theory and its role in scientific practice leads to lack of understanding both of the phenomenon of communication and of the process of investigation. Isolated and even contradictory findings, which tell us very little about communication, is a likely outcome of this state of affairs. After all, facts are not objects which must simply be unearthed; facts are interpretations and interpretations are based on and derive from theory. However, in trying to understand communication, theory must not be elevated to a *sui generis* status. Since it is an interpretation of reality, the investigator must at all times retain the vital link between theory and reality.

The foregoing arguments accentuate the need for recognising the theoretical approach that guides any particular investigation and for being aware of its limitations. To be able to make meaningful decisions concerning theoretical approaches and theories emanating from them, it is imperative to know the purpose and scope of available approaches. Consequently this monograph aims at introducing the reader to some of the most useful theoretical approaches to communication and to illustrate them with reference to representative theories which embody their assumptions. Since the approaches and theories discussed represent the field of *general communication theory*, this field is subsequently delimited and a classification of some of its most important theoretical approaches is suggested.

1.3 THE FIELD OF GENERAL COMMUNICATION THEORY

1.3.1 Introduction

Theoretical approaches to communication not only cover a broad field; the borderlines of the field are fluid, since various criteria may be used to delimit them. For the purposes of this monograph three criteria apply.

First, the chosen approaches represent "general" communication theory, that is, theoretical approaches concerning the phenomenon of communication as such, its constituent parts, defining characteristics and condition or quality at a given time and place. Theoretical approaches dealing with specialisation areas, such as print media, advertising and film, are thus excluded. In a sense the latter are dependent on the former. General communication theory establishes the phenomenon of communication in that it describes its nature and determines those characteristics that distinguish it from other phenomena. In contrast, "specialised" theory deals with individual parts, aspects, forms or specific kinds of communication. Each of these is considered a field of study in its own right because, in addition to its general communicological characteristics, it has unique features of its own.

Second, since they are not all purely or exclusively communicological in origin, the chosen approaches offer insight into several aspects of the multi-faceted phenomenon of communication. Apart from the fact that the borderlines between different social sciences are not absolute and rigid, the complexity of the phenomenon of communication forces investigators to consider it from various viewpoints. It is thus not surprising to find that general communication theory has borrowed several approaches from other disciplines. However, the authors have limited the range of approaches discussed by including only well-known approaches and ones that show potential for enriching our understanding of communication. Individual chapters in the monograph explain the choice of the approaches considered and the representative theories discussed to illustrate their view of communication.

Third, given the above definition of general communication theory, the chosen approaches do not apply to any specific setting or form of communication as such. However, most of the approaches discussed, lean more towards mass than towards interpersonal communication. The pervasive and decisive influence of mass communication in the modern Western world has simply forced communicologists to develop theory to deal with it. And some approaches and theories, which were originally designed for interpersonal communication, were later extended to include mass communication as well and/or to critically assess its quality.

1.3.2 A classification of general communication theory

Since various possible criteria may be used, no classification of general communication theory is final, universal or exhaustive. Each classification is made for a particular purpose and, depending on the criteria used, the same approach may be put into different categories.

In order to cover as many approaches as possible, this monograph suggests two main categories, each of which may be subdivided in turn. Theoretical approaches to communication offer either a view of the *phenomenon of communication as such*, or a *critical appraisal of its condition or quality* at a given time and place. Generally speaking, approaches dealing with the phenomenon as such, are concerned with what may be regarded as the essence of communication, while those that assess the quality of communication usually investigate and assess a specific example of the phenomenon by using an image of an/the ideal state of affairs as yardstick.

Each of the above categories may in turn be subdivided. Available approaches to the *phenomenon of communication* suggest three foci, namely the entire structure of the phenomenon, or a constituent part of the structure; the internal operation of the communication process in systems; and the dynamics of communication as a process of the constitution of meaning.

"Structure" normally refers to the mutual relationships between constituent parts of a phenomenon. Individual components as such are not investigated, but are only seen in relation to the whole structure. Functionalism, which offers the best illustration of this kind of approach, is discussed in Chapter 2, Section 2.2. The theory of De Fleur and Ball-Rokeach serves as a representative example.

While some approaches presuppose the existence of a structure, they only investigate a specific part of it, that is, they approach communication from the viewpoint of *one* of its constituent parts. To keep the classification as simple as possible, only three components are taken into consideration for the purposes of this monograph.

Approaches which stress the role of the *communicator* include examples such as rhetorical and persuasive approaches, behaviourism, the "balance theories" and some varieties of existentialism. In Chapter 2, Section 2.3 this category is defined and illustrated with reference to Kierkegaard's existentialist theory of direct/indirect communication.

Approaches which focus on the *medium* are best represented by media determinism. Chapter 2, Section 2.4 delimits this category of approaches and explains McLuhan's theory as a representative example.

Finally, approaches that accentuate the role of the *recipient* include examples such as hermeneutics and approaches dealing with the recipient's aesthetic experience. This category is defined and Gadamer's hermeneutical theory is discussed as a representative example in Chapter 2, Section 2.5.

Approaches dealing with communication from the viewpoint of the *internal operation* of communication systems, define communication as a process of information flow and examine the technical aspects of the transmission and exchange of information. (Mathematical) information theory, cybernetics and general system theory are examples of this category of approaches. Chapter 3 examines the latter two approaches.

Approaches that focus on the *dynamics* of communication also consider communication as a process, but in their notion of "process" they stress the continuous and ever-evolving constitution and exchange of meaning between participants. Any "structure" which communication may display, evolves from the process itself and cannot be determined beforehand. Given this unique and everchanging character of communication, "dynamics" (rather than "process") depicts the focus of these approaches. Approaches such as symbolic interactionism (defined and illustrated with reference to Goffman's theory in Chapter 4, Section 4.2), phenomenology (defined and illustrated with reference to Schutz's theory in Chapter 4, Section 4.3), some varieties of existentialism (defined and illustrated with reference to Buber's theory in Chapter 4, Section 4.4) and semiology (defined and illustrated with reference to some of its founders in Chapter 4, Section 4.5) may be placed in this group.

The second main group of theoretical approaches comprises those that *critically assess* the condition of the phenomenon of communication. By using a particular notion of a desired state of affairs as yardstick, these approaches try to determine what is wrong with the quality of communication, why this is the case and how the problem may be rectified. Existing approaches suggest two main subdivisions in this category.

Neo-Marxist and other critical approaches assess the quality of communication by investigating the social and/or cultural conditions in which it takes place and by examining their decisive consequences for the quality of participants' existence. Chapter 5 delimits this category of approaches and examines the representative theories of Orwell, Marcuse, Mills, Williams and Ellul.

Existentialist approaches assess the quality of communication by investigating individual participation in communication. While conceding that the social and cultural circumstances in which communication takes place may significantly influence opportunities for individual participation and appropriation of meaning in communication, these approaches emphasise individual responsibility for determining the quality of existence. Chapter 6 deals with this category and discusses the representative theories of Kierkegaard, Buber and Ortega y Gasset.

1.4 SUMMARY

In this chapter some of the misunderstanding concerning the concept of theory was clarified. It was shown that theory consists of different components and that different levels of theorising may be distinguished. Brief mention was made of some concepts normally used in conjunction with theory and the indispensable role of theory in scientific practice was highlighted. Finally, the field of general communication theory was delimited and a classification of some of its major theoretical approaches was offered. Some of these approaches, as well as representative theories which illustrate their view of communication, are examined in the remainder of the monograph.

Chapter 2

Theoretical approaches concerning the structure of communication

2.1 INTRODUCTION

Theoretical approaches discussed in this chapter, like those in Chapters 3 and 4, deal specifically with the phenomenon of communication. When communication is approached by way of its structure, either the entire structure or a particular part of it is the focus of attention, while other aspects or matters concerning communication are not investigated in their own right.

Theoretical approaches dealing with the entire structure of communication offer a genuine structural view of the phenomenon. Although individual parts are identified, the mutual relationships among them and the need for maintaining their interdependence to ensure the efficient operation and survival of the whole, are emphasised. The best-known and most complete example of this kind of approach is functionalism (see Section 2.2 below).

Some theoretical approaches assume that communication consists of several parts and that some kind of interrelationship obtains between them. A particular kind of interrelationship may even be posited. But, in their investigation of the phenomenon, they single out for study *one* of the constituent parts. In some cases the focus may imply an overemphasis on the chosen part (media determinism, discussed in Section 2.4, is a case in point), while in other cases approaches simply highlight the nature and significance of that particular part for the phenomenon of communication as a whole. Sections 2.3 to 2.5 deal, respectively, with approaches that focus on the communicator, medium and recipient.

2.2 FUNCTIONALISM

2.2.1 Introduction

Functionalism, one of the oldest approaches to mass communication, was a major shaping force in social scientific discourse for nearly a decade. It is still popular for certain purposes, notably in the fields of planning and policy-making. The subsequent discussion introduces important assumptions of functionalism, examines the theory of De Fleur and Ball-Rokeach, which is the most complete example of a functionalist theory, and offers some critical comments concerning the value of functionalism. A more detailed discussion of this approach appears in Jansen (1989: 14-27).

2.2.2 Some assumptions of functionalism

Functionalist interest in the structure of communication is evident in its major assumption, namely that the phonomenon of mass communication is a system, that is, a whole consisting of several interrelated and interdependent parts. Although functionalists distinguish various individual parts of communication, such as communicators, messages, media organisations and recipients, the significance of each part derives, not from its own peculiar characteristics, but from its position in relation to the other parts of the system.

Each part of the system fulfils a function, that is, makes a contribution to the smooth functioning and maintenance of the entire system. When all individual parts properly fulfil their functions, the system is in balance (equilibrium). The system can only accommodate minor changes, such as minor deviations from the proper fulfilment of a prescribed function, while drastic or fundamental change constitutes a threat to the survival of the system. Attempts to counteract deviant tendencies, in order to return the system to a state of balance, may take on various forms.

The assumption of self-regulation is closely related to that of goal-attainment. The ultimate goal of the system is self-preservation and all system functions are geared to this overall purpose.

A system may form part of a larger system. Hence the boundaries of a given system must be clearly demarcated. It is maintained that a system may be distinguished from its environment by the intensity of relationships among its constituent parts.

The system postulated by functionalism is almost lifeless, for the human beings in the system have no significance other than their specified functions towards the survival of the system. If they deviate, control mechanisms and corrective measures bring them back in line.

2.2.3 De Fleur and Ball-Rokeach's theory

The American authors, De Fleur and Ball-Rokeach (1975), consider mass communication as a system in its own right and as a subsystem of society. They are primarily interested in how the mass media maintain a state of equilibrium and manage to survive.

Each mass medium consists of several interdependent parts, such as producers, the audience, research organisations and advertising agencies. The separate mass media are, in turn, interrelated and form the system of mass communication in society. The mass communication system exists in an environment which includes other parts of society, for example legal organisations and the economic subsystem. The maintenance of equilibrium in the system is dependent on the satisfaction of the basic system needs and the authors maintain that system needs are fulfilled by stable and repetitive behavioural patterns that occur in the system.

The primary need of the mass communication system is money which is supplied by the audience. Since any drastic change in audience behaviour therefore constitutes a threat to the stability of the system, it must be prevented at all costs. Hence the mass media constantly seek to provide the kind of content which will satisfy the largest possible number of audience members so that they will continue to pay for the programmes.

De Fleur and Ball-Rokeach locate the crucial stable and repetitive element in the mass media in so-called "low-taste content", that is, programmes of low artistic and moral quality which are distributed to large numbers of recipients. According to the authors low-taste content satisfies the audience and motivates them to pay for the programmes because it confirms their basic beliefs. Thus, there is little chance that the equilibrium of the mass communication system, or the status quo of society, will be disturbed. It is clear that the recipient within the system is a mere cog in the wheel and is important only in as far as he/she keeps on paying for low-taste content.

2.2.4 Critical assessment

De Fleur and Ball-Rokeach's contribution lies mainly in the illustration of the functionalist view offered by their description of the American mass communication system. Although they may be criticised for matters such as their definition of low-taste content and their insistence on money as the primary system need, the more serious limitations, as well as the contributions, of their theory derive from its functionalist nature.

Like any theoretical approach, functionalism offers a limited view of communication which is useful for certain purposes only. For instance, functionalism offers insight into the complex inter-relationships between mass communication and the other parts of society and the ways in which mass communication is influenced by and, in turn, influences the social structure. Due to its concern for counteracting deviant tendencies, functionalism highlights possible sources of malfunctioning in communication systems and offers insight into the operation of such systems. Hence it may yield guidelines for the efficient operation of systems. Finally, function-alism offers an overview of the different parts of a mass communi-cation system and their interrelationships.

The functionalist view of "a smoothly-running system in equilibrium" does not merely offer a description of a particular kind of communication. For the functionalist this description captures the essence of communication and thus shows the ideal state of affairs that should be sought after. Hence functionalism has often been accused of serving as justification for the status quo.

Closely related to its conservative bias is the inferior role that functionalism attributes to the human being. In fact, in the functionalist system the human being is at the mercy of forces beyond his/her control and can hardly initiate change in the system. In addition, the human being's needs are subordinate to those of the system and it is of no concern to the functionalist whether or not the system is of any positive significance in the lives of real people.

2.3 THEORETICAL APPROACHES CONCERNING THE COMMUNICATOR

2.3.1 Introduction

Theoretical approaches which examine communication from the viewpoint of the communicator (see Chapter 1, Section 1.3.2 for examples) show great variety and do not subscribe to the same view of communication. Generally speaking, they share the following characteristics.

Approaches in this category focus not only on the position of the communicator in relation to the other components of communication, but in particular on the shaping influence of the communicator in the process of communication. The communicator initiates communication to achieve certain "results"; hence he/she plans to steer the whole process and to intervene, where necessary, to ensure the desired outcome. However, approaches in this category differ with reference to matters such as the qualities of the communicator and his/her attitude towards the recipient, the way in which the communicator should proceed, the role and nature of the recipient's involvement in communication, the desired outcome of communication and the communicator and recipient's responsibility for the outcome of their encounter.

For most approaches in this category the communicator is a recognisable person or may be associated with an institution. However, in cases such as behaviourism and congruence or balance theory, the "communicator" is rather elusive, since the presence of an "external influence", which significantly affects the recipient's behaviour, is emphasised.

To illustrate this category of approaches, Kierkegaard's theory of direct/indirect communication is discussed below. (Since this theory represents an existentialist approach Section 4.4.1 in Chapter 4, which defines existentialism for the purposes of this monograph, should be read in conjunction with the discussion below.)

2.3.2 Kierkegaard's theory

The Danish philosopher and father of existentialism, Søren Aabye Kierkegaard (1813-1855), is considered one of the most influential thinkers of the West. His life's work revolves around the meaning of human existence. Although he sketches a great variety of existential possibilities, he is essentially a religious author for whom existence ultimately means "to become a Christian" (Kierkegaard 1962: 15-21). In comparison with most of the authors in this category, communication is for Kierkegaard not merely an exercise in persuasion or manipulation but, first and foremost, a mode of existence.

Kierkegaard's best-known publications include *Either-or* (1843), *Stages on life's way* (1845), *Concluding unscientific postscript* (1846), *Works of love* (1847) and *Training in Christianity* (1850).

Kierkegaard's communication theory lays stress on the communicator, medium and recipient. However, given the circumstances surrounding the rise of mass communication in his day, he finds that the recipient is increasingly subjected to communication which offers little, if any, opportunity for personal appropriation of the message (see Chapter 6, Section 6.2.2 for a discussion of his critique of mass communication). Since the problem stems from the way in which communicators approach recipients, his direct/indirect mode of communication highlights the role of the communicator in helping the recipient to become actively involved in appropriation of meaning.

2.3.2.1 Kierkegaard's assumptions concerning communication

For Kierkegaard communication is a mode of existence by which each and every individual human being may authentically express him/herself. "Existence" bears the connotation of distinguishing oneself from others, not in the sense of egotistically elevating oneself above other people, but in the sense of making an imprint on the world (Lowrie 1942: 171). Kierkegaard explains this viewpoint in his concept of the single individual (*den Enkelte*): human existence is authentic to the extent that it is expressive of each and every person's individuality. The meaning of human life is not determined collectively, but by personal appropriation of meaning. (For a more complete discussion of the single individual see Kierkegaard 1962: 109-138.)

However, the individual person is not a recluse. To become a single individual is a lifelong process that requires not only constantly becoming aware of oneself, but constantly actualising oneself. And for Kierkegaard self-actualisation takes place through self-expression in communication with others, in which case the self acknowledges and affirms the other person's self as well.

The self is a synthesis of contraries, the most important being the temporal and the eternal, finitude and infinity and necessity and freedom. The task of actualising oneself is the task of finding ways to reconcile the contraries in oneself. The opposites are dialectically related to one another and the antitheses are never suspended. Since the individual human being cannot tolerate the contradictions within him/herself, he/she is constantly faced with a choice between various possible combinations of contraries, that is, various possible ways of existing. Each way of existing reveals a particular level of self-actualisation.

Closely related to the concept of the self is that of spheres of existence. Kierkegaard's three principal spheres, namely the aesthetic, ethical and religious, may be approached from two viewpoints. On the one hand, a sphere of existence entails a lifeview concerning self-actualisation while, on the other hand, it refers to the expression of that lifeview in a particular form of communication, such as manipulation or dialogue. Different levels of self-actualisation may be distinguished in every sphere of existence and different spheres may overlap in a single person's life. Although Kierkegaard does not propose a fixed progression from one sphere to the next, the aesthetic sphere involves the least self-actualisation and the religious sphere the most. A more complete discussion of the self and the spheres of existence is given by Jansen (1986).

Kierkegaard's views concerning communication serve as yardstick in his assessment of the quality of mass communication (see Chapter 6, Section 6.2.2). To be able to understand the nature of direct/indirect communication and Kierkegaard's purpose with these modes of communication, it should be noted that he considers lack of individual self-expression as the major problem of his day. As a result of various historical developments, life became collective and, when everyone resembled everyone else, no one was confronted with alternative modes of existence and a need to choose between them.

Kierkegaard examines the recipient in mass communication, but is particularly concerned about the average churchgoer who, in his opinion, knows the contents of the Christian message but does not appropriate its meaning, because the way in which it is communicated does not invite personal involvement. Hence Kierkegaard's direct/indirect communication (showing clearly the influence of Socrates), which was designed to awaken the recipient by presenting him/her with contraries between which he/she has to choose. It should be noted in passing that Kierkegaard's carefully planned and structured oeuvre as a whole works dialectically.

2.3.2.2 Direct/indirect communication

Kierkegaard's choice between either, or a combination of, direct and indirect communication is not a simple matter. His authorship bears witness to his lifelong struggle to determine the most suitable way of expressing himself. Initially he favoured the indirect mode, which is best represented by his so-called pseudonymous works in which poetised characters introduce a variety of existential possibilities. However, each pseudonymous work was accompanied by a discourse or discourses published under his own name. In the latter he used both direct and indirect communication. Towards the end of his life he predominantly used direct communication, a possible reason being that he thought indirect communication had not sufficiently awakened the recipient and that a direct message concerning his/her existential condition was the last resort.

Direct communication is the communication of knowledge (Kierkegaard 1967: entry 651,B). Since it involves a straightforward statement as to what a particular matter is all about, Kierkegaard regards direct communication as a suitable mode for conveying knowledge hitherto unknown to the recipient. Direct communication centres on the contents of the message and the knowledge conveyed has the same meaning for all recipients. It is normally used for transmitting scientific knowledge, but Kierkegaard notes that direct communication may also be used for initially acquainting the recipient with the contents of the Christian message (Kierkegaard 1967: entry 653, 29).

However, when the recipient knows the contents of the (Christian) message, but has been misguided as to its meaning, the illusion must be removed to restore the recipient's ability to receive the message. For this purpose an entirely different mode of communication is required (Kierkegaard 1962: 24;40). Indirect communication involves the placing together of dialectical contrasts without offering any explanation that may influence the recipient's interpretation (Kierkegaard 1967: entry 679 and Kierkegaard 1962: 25). An indirect communication presents the recipient with a riddle for which all alternative interpretations are equally possible. Without any guidance as to what alternative may be chosen, the recipient is forced to choose for him/herself by self-consciously appropriating the message. Thus, in contrast to direct communication, indirect communication involves knowledge peculiar to each individual recipient, that is, self-knowledge.

In indirect communication the communicator ensures that the recipient acts independently. The communicator does offer the recipient some help by introducing him/her to contradictory alternatives, but the absence of guidance as to his/her choice ensures that in this maieutic relationship the end result is determined, not by the communicator, but by the recipient. The communicator is in fact "absent" from his/her communication.

Kierkegaard uses irony and humour to present an indirect communication. The ambiguous form of such a communication not only invites more than one interpretation, but deceives the recipient as to the real purpose of the communication. Since the communicator appears to be jesting while he/she is serious, or vice versa, the recipient does not consider the communicator an honest person and he/she is lured into an existential exercise carefully planned by the communicator (Kierkegaard 1967: entry 649, 24).

It should be noted that indirect communication is ethical in that it helps the recipient to express him/herself (Kierkegaard 1967: entry 650, 12). It does not involve manipulation of the recipient and the latter is not persuaded to accept the communicator's viewpoint. In recognising his/her own existential condition, it is the recipient that persuades him/herself to choose an alternative way of existing. The communicator's role is merely to make the recipient aware of alternative possibilities.

Apart from the principles on which direct/indirect communication is based, Kierkegaard's writings offer the communicator guidelines for existential communication, a few of which are mentioned below. Jansen (in Perkins 1990) offers a more detailed exposition of Kierkegaard's principles.

Although he uses a mass medium, Kierkegaard addresses each recipient individually by, for example, using personal forms of address and, in particular, by telling him/her something of significance to his/her life. To be able to do so, Kierkegaard addresses his message to a particular kind of recipient. He never wrote for anyone who might be interested, but for an intended recipient of whose existential condition he was aware. Not only does he know his intended recipient, he meets him/her where he/she is, existentially speaking (Kierkegaard 1962: 27-29).

Kierkegaard often applies the principles of repetition and variety. Not only is his message repeated in several publications, it is presented from different viewpoints. Thus he both elucidates the existential possibilities concerned and ensures that the recipient remains interested in the message. To prevent too many possibilities from distracting the recipient's attention, he employs the principle of "narrowing". For example, Kierkegaard deliberately planned his oeuvre to gradually lead the recipient from temporal concerns to those things that mattered in Christian existence.

Kierkegaard's viewpoint that the *way* in which a message is conveyed is crucial in determining its meaning for recipients is, for example, illustrated by the different kinds of publications and the various styles and designs that he used. He was aware of the importance of the medium used in communication and proved to be versatile in his use of it.

2.3.2.3 Critical assessment

To gain a more complete understanding of Kierkegaard's most important communicological contributions, this section should be read in conjunction with Chapter 6, Section 6.2.3 which deals with his assessment of mass communication.

Kierkegaard allows for different forms of communication and shows that communication may be used for different purposes. Although he did not know how society and mass communication would develop, he realised that, in a complex society, mass communication would be used for various purposes.

However, by posing an inseparable link between communication and existence, Kierkegaard shows that communication is, first and foremost, a mode of existence which reveals the quality of existence. By sketching a variety of existential possibilities, each of which is actualised through communication, he offers a multi-dimensional view of human life. Although he did not develop the dialectical principle, he shows that it is crucial to an understanding of the ever-changing character of human existence and he offers extensive illustrations of its operation and significance in human life. However, his viewpoint that Christian existence involves the highest level of self-actualisation is somewhat limiting, since not all human beings adopt the Christian faith.

An important insight, although not original to Kierkegaard, is that communication has existential significance for participants only when they personally appropriate the meaning of the encounter. Hence the quality of communication itself is determined by individual participation. Kierkegaard emphasises the active participation of both communicator and recipient. However, in his day, the recipient's participation had to be evoked by the communicator. Kierkegaard is one of the first modern authors to demonstrate how a communicator may involve recipients in *mass* communication by "absenting" him/herself from the communication.

Kierkegaard is widely recognised as a master of irony and humour, the two principal ways in which he tried to awaken the self-activation of recipients. Likewise, his skilful use of pseudonyms is considered an outstanding contribution. Kierkegaard only demonstrated the use of indirect and combined direct/indirect communication in one mass medium, and the question as to how they may be employed in other mass media has yet to be explored.

Apart from determining how his sound communicological principles may be applied and the potentialities of the different mass media explored for this purpose, communicators may well consider Kierkegaard's crucial insight, namely that the "effect" of the message on the recipient is determined by the *way* in which it is conveyed, rather than by its contents.

Finally, it should be noted that Kierkegaard's theory of direct/ indirect communication is not merely an intellectual exercise. His genuine concern for his fellow human beings marks him as a humanist thinker and accentuates the responsibility of the communicator for constantly assessing the consequences of his/her communication for recipients. By emphasising the crucial role of the recipient in determining the meaning of a message for his/her life Kierkegaard, in turn, highlights the responsibility of the recipient and suggests a way by which recipients may critically assess messages directed at them.

2.4 THEORETICAL APPROACHES CONCERNING THE MEDIUM

2.4.1 Introduction

The medium is usually defined as the technical or physical means whereby messages are transmitted in the communication process. The medium thus provides the necessary link between communicator and recipient. Theoretical approaches which are concerned with the medium range in scope from the study of spoken language and nonverbal behaviour (gestures, facial expressions, etc.) to the mechanical and electronic mass media (radio, films, television, newspapers). These approaches have in common that they consider the medium to play a more important role in the communication process than simply the bearer of messages between the participants. The medium itself is seen to have an influential role in how the message is formulated and understood. The main focus is often directed at ways in which a particular medium can assist the communicator to deliver a more effective (persuasive) message and/or the effects of the message on the recipient.

Theoretical approaches which overemphasise the medium as the most important component in communication are known as media determinism. Such approaches tend to minimise the role of people in creating and interpreting meaning, and ascribe to the media the power of influencing not only the message, but society itself. To illustrate this category of approaches Marshall McLuhan's theory is discussed below.

McLuhan, who coined the phrase "the medium is the message" (1974:15), is probably the best known contemporary writer about media effects. Although McLuhan is interested in all communication media, he is renowned for his views on the technology and power of modern electronic media to shape society.

McLuhan's views are scattered throughout his various writings, and the explanations that he offers for his many controversial statements about the media are often incomplete and difficult to understand. The authors acknowledge the valuable contribution to the following discussion made by Tom Wolfe's lucid summary (in Stearn 1968).

2.4.2 McLuhan's theory

Marshall McLuhan (1911-1980) was a Canadian literary and communications scholar who enjoyed widespread fame in the 1960s for his work on the social and cultural implications of the mass media. McLuhan took his doctorate in English at Cambridge and spent most of his life as a teacher at American and Canadian universities. Until shortly before his death, he was director of the Institute for Cultural Studies in Toronto. His most important ideas on communication are contained in *The Gutenberg galaxy: the making of typographic man* (1962), *Understanding media: the extensions of man* (1974), first published in 1964, and (with Fiore) *The medium is the massage* (1967). During the 1980s a renewed interest in historical studies of the mass media inspired new interest in McLuhan's work. The subsequent discussion is based mainly on McLuhan's *Understanding media: the extensions of man*.

2.4.2.1 McLuhan's assumptions about communication

McLuhan's interest in communication was sparked off by the work of fellow academics and scientists on the critical importance of physical communications in a country as vast and sparsely populated as Canada. His particular interest in the characteristics of communication media began in the 1940s while studying popular culture. He was particularly interested in the way that advertisements and newspapers achieve their effects. He describes this as a mosaic of impressions created by the juxtaposition of pictures, words, colours, different typefaces, and so on which invite participation by the recipient in the communication experience. This assumption led him to examine the form — in preference to the content — of all the different media that exist in society. He came to regard the content of messages as irrelevant and emphasised the determinative role of the medium and its technology on society: any new medium constitutes a new environment which controls what people do, and how they think and act. McLuhan's concept of "medium" is broad; in addition to communication media, it also includes modes of transportation and the new communications technologies.

2.4.2.2 The medium is the message

"The medium is the message" (McLuhan 1974:15) is the main proposition in his theory. He continually emphasises that the medium has a greater influence than the content of what is communicated. The message of television, for example, is not what is seen on the set, but what effect television has had on the culture, and how it has changed the people and the society. The message is structured in terms of the medium; therefore, the medium and not content, constitutes the message.

The core of McLuhan's theory is that people adapt to their environment through a certain balance or ratio of the senses. The primary medium of an age brings out a particular sense ratio. He explains that all media are extensions of our senses and our functions. Man has developed extensions for practically everything that he used to do with his body. The wheel is an extension of the foot, writing an extension of sight, clothes an extension of the skin, electronic circuits an extension of the central nervous system, and so on (McLuhan & Fiore 1967). Each medium exaggerates a particular sense and leads to new modes of perception, new types of sensory experiences, and finally new relationships with the environment and other people.

Every major technology changes the balance between the senses and influences the way in which we perceive the world. McLuhan explains how writing, then printing, and today television, have transformed our culture. Before printing was invented, people communicated through speech, a form of communication not dissimilar to preliterate tribal societies. The sense of hearing was dominant. McLuhan maintains that hearing-oriented communities tend to receive and express many experiences simultaneously. They are in touch with every aspect of the environment and with each other. People who get their information from other people are necessarily closer together. They are also more emotional — the spoken word conveys anger, sorrow, joy and so on, with greater intensity than the printed word.

The mechanical developments of the industrial revolution brought about a radical change. People began getting their information primarily by seeing it. The printed word brought a new sense ratio into being in which sight predominated. This caused a bias in human perception. McLuhan proposes that Western culture as we know it today developed because the nature of print forced people into a linear, logical and categorical kind of perception, rather like the string of words and letters on the printed page. Print also converts audible sounds into abstract symbols (the letters of the alphabet). McLuhan believes that the result of the visual and spatial emphasis of the printed word has had detrimental effects on the other sense organs. In his words, visual people have substituted "an eye for an ear" (McLuhan 1974: 91). They are communicologically "deaf" — out of touch with the environment and detached from each other.

Today, new technologies are causing yet another change. They have ushered in a new electronic age in which the aural sense is again predominant. Although modern man is literate, people obtain most of their information by hearing it — primarily through electronic sources such as the telephone, radio and television. McLuhan sees in the electronic circuit a similarity to the human nervous system. The electronic media stimulate perception by all the senses and thereby restore sensory equilibrium. They have put us back in touch with the environment and with other people.

McLuhan's explanation of the effects of the medium on the senses is linked to the division he makes between "hot" and "cool" media, terms which refer to the "temperature" of the information or the "definition" of the image (1974: 31). The temperature of a message is not to be confused with its content. McLuhan classifies media and their messages in terms of the degree to which they involve people perceptually. Hot media contain relatively complete sensory data so that the informational content of the message is high or hot. Hot media such as print thus require minimal participation from the recipient — the meaning is delivered in the message itself. Cool media, on the other hand, require the individual to participate perceptually by filling in missing sensory data.

The comparison between film and television that McLuhan makes, elucidates the difference (1974: 329-360). Film is a hot medium because the image projected on the screen is three-dimensional, complete in every detail, and the viewer is not required to fill in missing information in order to understand the message. A television shot is cool because it has very low definition; it is two-dimensional, rather like a comicstrip cartoon. Television requires the viewer to participate in obtaining information by filling in the spaces and contours with his mind, as he does with a cartoon. The viewer is therefore more involved in the television image than the film image. McLuhan suggests that when our eyes look at things on television, they behave as if they were handling or touching the image. They seem to rub over it, filling in the mosaic of impressions. In this way, we participate in understanding television images.

The distinction between hot and cool media is crucial because of the different impact which they have on society. Because the meaning in a hot message is complete, it creates a dulling or hypnosis in the senses of the population, whereas a cool medium stimulates the senses. McLuhan defines Western culture as hot, while primitive or underdeveloped cultures are cool. He maintains that we are presently in transition from a hot culture to a cool culture. The change is created by the media that we use for communication — books are being replaced by television and the computer, for example, and the augmented participation required by the recipients creates a new type of society which in certain respects is similar to the tribal life of cool cultures, only now on a global scale.

The modern world has become a global village in which our thoughts, actions, institutions, and our relationship to society and to each other have been modified by the electronic media. Television technology, particularly satellite transmission, makes possible the instantaneous, worldwide dissemination of information, culture, values and attitudes. Time and distance are bridged so that what is happening in countries thousands of kilometres away can be observed in one's own home, much like the situation in a small village where little happens that is not known to everybody. The change is not without problems — it creates tremendous stresses in society while people adjust during the transition. For example, the new environment is reshaping the perceptual life of the young, but the modern acoustic child is still confronted in the classroom by teachers who think in a linear fashion. For McLuhan the resulting perceptual confusion is a "crippling factor in the learning process today" (1974: 356), particularly for children in transitional Western cultures. He believes that not until the next generation will society fully reap the benefits of the electronic age.

2.4.2.3 Critical assessment

During the 1960s, McLuhan was severely criticised for the incoherence of his ideas, his unsubstantiated and ambiguous statements, and the lack of evidence to support his psychological arguments. "His writing is deliberately antilogical: circular, repetitious, unqualified, gnomic, outrageous" (Elliott in Stearn 1968: 67) is a typical assessment. (The interested reader is referred to Littlejohn (1983: 268-269) for a selection of McLuhan's more controversial statements about various media.) Critics asserted that his views represent, at the very least, technological overdeterminism. He reduces people to things by ignoring their participation in the construction of meaning. Littlejohn (1983: 268) points out that his use of "participation" and "involvement" does not refer to the degree of interest or time spent attending to a particular medium; it refers to the completeness (hot) or incompleteness (cool) of the stimulus. In later years, however, McLuhan's view shifted somewhat, and he accorded people a greater personal role in the creation of meaning.

A neo-Marxist critic such as Raymond Williams (see Chapter 5, Section 5.5) is highly critical of the fact that McLuhan was not concerned with social and political problems. His study of technologies did not include any consideration of the social circumstances affecting their dissemination. His theory in fact conceals an ideological assumption — by maintaining that technology influences society, he ignores the fact that the ruling regime controls the technology.

Nevertheless, McLuhan had a strong following. His defence of the tirade against him is that "I am an investigator. I make probes. I have no point of view. I do not stay in one position . . . I don't explain — I explore" (McLuhan in Stearn 1968: xiii). While this may be a defence of his style and an indication of his desire to stimulate thought rather than make clear statements, it does not explain his theoretical position. McLuhan's theory, however, is not without merits. He certainly succeeded in stimulating people (including fellow-academics) to look at the media in a different way — hence the controversy.

His major contribution to the study of communication lies in his recognition of the scope, extent and impact of the media. Most media research studies emphasise the results of the message rather than the qualities of the media themselves. McLuhan has, for instance, made public speakers aware of how the characteristics of different mass media shape their personal images. Hitler, for example, who "electrocuted" the masses over the radio with his dramatic style of presentation, would have looked ridiculous on television. In contrast, television provided the ideal medium for conveying John Kennedy's more endearing personality, and has given the charismatic Billy Graham the greatest evangelical following in the world. The medium is the message?

2.5 THEORETICAL APPROACHES CONCERNING THE RECIPIENT

2.5.1 Introduction

Theoretical approaches which examine communication from the viewpoint of the recipient are generally directed at ways in which the recipient can overcome the emphasis that is often placed on the communicator's intentions (as in rhetorical or persuasive theories — see Chapter 1, Section 1.3.2) or the effects of the medium on the message (e.g. McLuhan's theory in Section 2.4 above). Recipient-oriented approaches do not regard the recipient as the passive receiver or end point of the communicator's message, but as an active and equal partner in the communication process. The emphasis is usually placed on the way in which the recipient interprets the message. He/she is expected to make a conscious effort to become subjectively involved in giving meaning to the message and to appropriate that meaning for his/her own life-world. In this way he/she is able to overcome the (often covert) manipulative elements in the message. The recipient him/herself is thus responsible for the outcome of the communication encounter.

The way in which interpretation takes place is the subject of hermeneutics. The particular theory of interpretation used to illustrate this section is the philosophical hermeneutics of the German philosopher, Hans-Georg Gadamer (1900-). (Since Gadamer's theory is closely related to both phenomenology and existentialism, Sections 4.3.1 and 4.4.1 in Chapter 4 which define phenomenology and existentialism respectively for the purpose of this monograph, should be read in conjunction with the discussion below.)

2.5.2 Gadamer's theory

Gadamer's views are based on those of his predecessor and mentor, Martin Heidegger (1889-1976), whose hermeneutical theory in

Being and time (1967), first published in German in 1927, he extended and enlarged. Gadamer's theory of interpretation is presented in Truth and method (1985), first published in German in 1960, and *Philosophical hermeneutics* (1977). Gadamer's theory has influenced not only philosophy, but several related disciplines including communication, history, literature and art. His views are particularly relevant to the study of communication as he draws an analogy between the process of interpretation and the process of communication. In this analogy, Gadamer considers the viewpoint of the recipient, rather than the intention of the communicator or the effects of the message.

2.5.2.1 Gadamer's assumptions about hermeneutics

Hermeneutics has its origins in biblical interpretation and the grammatical and linguistic rules that govern the translation of classical texts. The German hermeneutical tradition was established by Friedrich Schleiermacher (1768-1834) and Wilhelm Dilthey (1833-1911), whose theories were influenced by the seventeenth-century philosophy of rationalism. The belief at that time was that because the writer and interpreter of a text come from different historical and geographical backgrounds, the interpreter's present knowledge is the source of prejudices and distortions that cause him to misunderstand the author's meaning. To bridge the historical gap, the interpreter had to leave his present time and life-world and return to the past in order to reconstruct the author's feelings and intentions. For this purpose, scientific methods were used to establish objectively valid models whereby the author's mental processes could be reproduced by the interpreter. The meanings that were gleaned would be valid for all people and all time.

Gadamer critically questions these assumptions. His view is that human experiences cannot be scientifically validated. He is thus not concerned with presenting a methodology for correct interpretation, but with bringing people to an understanding of the role that they could play in interpreting the circumstances of their lives. Gadamer's alternative is not to search for the objective meaning in the text or to reconstruct the author's intention, but to enter into a conversation or dialogue with the text in which the reader's life-world is a necessary part of the process of understanding.

Although Gadamer uses the paradigm of the written text to explain his views, he proposes that as his theory is concerned with the activity of understanding in general, it is applicable to all situations which require interpretation. He shows how the recipient can appropriate personal meaning from communication messages (or "texts") by explaining his views on history, dialogue and language.

2.5.2.2 History, dialogue and language

Gadamer maintains that the interpreter's historical tradition and present life-world cannot be ignored — they play a constituent role in the process of understanding. Every interpreter always approaches the text with some knowledge or "pre-understanding" (Gadamer 1985: 235-239) of the subject matter addressed by the text. This knowledge arises from the culture or historical tradition into which he/she is born. His/her horizon of knowledge includes the assumptions or "prejudices" (Gadamer 1985: 245) about the world that have been inherited from his/her culture. Because this knowledge is part of his/her very existence, no interpreter can ever empty his/her mind and approach a text objectively. He/she always approaches it with a measure of understanding obtained from the past. Similarly, every text exists in the horizon of knowledge of the time in which it is created, and contains the prejudices of the author. Gadamer maintains that the meaning of the work will be revealed in relation to the interpreter's willingness to enter into a dialogue with the text during which the prejudices of both are questioned and mutual understanding about the subject matter of the text is reached.

Dialogue is defined as an open discussion in which the participants take part on an equal footing with the intention of reaching mutual understanding about the topic under discussion (cf. Johannesen 1971). Gadamer uses the Socratic method of dialogue as a model for the hermeneutical conversation. The Socratic dialogue is characterised by its dialectical structure: understanding of the subject matter is reached through the process of question and answer. The Socratic method requires that both participants in the dialogue acknowledge that their present knowledge is incomplete, and that their views are open to question. The to-and-fro movement of question and answer in the dialogue ensures that both participants remain dynamically involved in the conversation; both have the opportunity to express themselves and to interpret each other's message.

Gadamer (1985: 321) argues that understanding a text is analogous to understanding another person as the "thou" in the I-thou relationship of genuine dialogical communication (see Buber's views in Chapter 4, Section 4.4.2.2). This relationship is possible because the text is not an inanimate object — it carries meaning intentionally placed there by a fellow human being. The text contains not only the thoughts of the writer, but is an expression of his/her creative self, and thus embodies his/her experience of life. The reader's role is to imbue the text with a measure of life, so that it acquires an autonomous existence and "speaks" to the reader as the partner in dialogue. During this "conversation", the text reveals its inherent meaning. The understanding that is reached is thus not between reader and writer, but between reader and text. In Gadamer's theory, interpretation depends on the quality of the communication encounter between the individual reader and the text itself. The emphasis is on the interpretative role of the reader and his/her intention to participate actively in the dialogue, to "hear" the message that the text has to offer, and to make it meaningful within his/her own life-world. By interpreting what the text "says", reader and writer reach the goal of the dialogical encounter — mutual understanding.

The task of the reader (recipient) to bring the text out of its fixed written form into the movement of dialogue does not depend on a method to be followed by the reader, but on his/her active participation in the dialogue and the nature of the questions that he/she puts to the text. The conversation between the reader and the text, like all genuine dialogue, involves equality and equal reciprocity. Interpreter and text each stand in a horizon of knowledge in which is contained the prejudices of both. The interpretation begins as the reader initiates the dialogue by anticipating certain things on the basis of his/her pre-understanding, and proceeds as reader and text question each other. As the reader questions the text, his/her own horizon of knowledge expands to include that of the past, and as the text questions the reader, the reader's preconceptions and prejudices are challenged and either confirmed, discarded or altered.

Gadamer maintains that the text will reveal its life-world and "speak" to the reader provided that he/she opens him/herself to its "voice" and allows it to assert its point of view. At the same time, he/she is not a passive partner in the dialogue. What the text "says" to him/her, will depend on the type of questions that he/she is able to ask. Gadamer (1985: 330-331) explains that the Socratic art of questioning is not to out-argue the other in order to "win". The art is to bring out the truth of the subject matter, to reveal its possibilities and not to allow it to be overtaken by the opinion of one partner. What then emerges is the truth of the subject matter, which belongs to neither participant, but transcends the subjective opinions of both. It is the responsibility of the reader not to impose his/her subjective opinions onto the text and, simultaneously, not to allow the text's horizon of knowledge to absorb his/her own. The interaction between reader and text is an intersubjective relationship in which two life-worlds meet. Without destroying the perceptions of each other, the horizons of interpreter and text are fused into a common view of the subject matter.

Gadamer substantiates his contention that understanding is reached between reader and text, and not reader and author, by explaining his view of language. He rejects theories which regard language as a "tool" which people invented in order to exchange information (1985: 364). In his view, the world is linguistic in nature. Language as a concept existed before it was spoken by any one individual. Words thus arise from the situation or experience in which they are spoken. Language therefore bears its own truth within it and by sharing in it, people are able to attribute meaning to the world around them and to express these meanings to others. Since language does not "belong" to the individual, meaning can never be "fixed" into a text by the author. The text reveals its own meaning in a dialogical encounter with the reader. The text itself speaks to the reader, so that understanding is not of language (as in scientific hermeneutics) but through language. Interpretation means that the reader understands the text, not the author, because it is the text that articulates the author's understanding of his/her existence in the world.

Gadamer argues that our ability to understand at all is the achievement of language. We internalise our experiences and thoughts in the form of unspoken words in order to explain them to ourselves. Everything that is intelligible and that can be understood and interpreted has an inherently linguistic nature. We understand art, music and our everyday experiences in the world because we have language in which to express our understanding. For this reason, Gadamer maintains that hermeneutics is not only concerned with the interpretation of the written word; its scope encompasses the interpretation of every aspect of our existence in the world.

Gadamer's conclusion is that interpretation is not the reconstruction of the author's intention, but a new event, "a new creation of understanding" (1985: 419) which comes into being during dialectical interaction between the interpreter and the text. Gadamer does not suggest that every new interpretation is absolutely different from what the author intended or from how his/her own time understood him/her. It means that meaning is always open, it remains a possibility. Each reader is an individual with a life-world of his/her own. Therefore, for every reader there could be a different interpretation, a new event in understanding.

2.5.2.3 Critical assessment

Gadamer's most distinctive contribution to contemporary interpretation theory is his reconceptualisation of hermeneutics as the understanding, not only of written texts, but of all "texts" which require interpretation — literature, art, music, philosophy, history, everyday experiences, and even the meaning of human existence. Although he does not specifically discuss the conditions of interpersonal or mass communication, the close analogy that he draws between communication and hermeneutics leads to a deeper understanding of the interpretation process in communication encounters. By including all the arts as "texts", Gadamer highlights the function of the arts in society as communication media which play a significant role in helping people to reach an understanding of the world. Most importantly, his in-depth analysis of the interpretative role of the recipient helps to change the stereotyped image of the passive recipient (particularly in mass communication) dancing to the communicator's tune. Gadamer makes it clear, however, that the responsibility for maintaining the communication process in dynamic equilibrium rests with the recipient.

Gadamer is criticised for the overemphasis that he places on the recipient's subjective involvement in interpretation, and his neglect of the communicator's intentions, which invalidates the possibility of an "objective" interpretation. The opposite view is equally tenable — that taking only the communicator's viewpoint into account and excluding the recipient's appropriation of meaning, leads to an equally one-sided interpretation. A close reading of Gadamer's theory shows that he implicitly suggests that understanding is a process of negotiation between reader and writer through the text (the fusion of horizons). The problem lies in his assertion that it is the text, not the author, that determines its meaning. Jürgen Habermas, for example, criticises Gadamer's insistence on the autonomy and universality of language in knowledge and understanding because Gadamer overlooks the social determinants of knowledge, such as power relations, which give language an ideological function in society (Habermas in How 1980).

In conclusion, Gadamer's theory serves to substantiate that a comprehensive theory needs to take into account all the components that constitute the communication process, including the social context in which it takes place.

2.6 SUMMARY

In this chapter the reader was introduced to theoretical approaches which describe communication from the viewpoint of its structure or a constituent part of its structure. Each approach was illustrated with reference to a well-known representative theory which embodies the assumptions of the approach. A critical assessment of the theories showed some of the contributions and shortcomings of the views of communication offered by the theoretical approaches concerned. The next chapter deals with approaches to the process of communication within systems. —>

Chapter 3

Theoretical approaches concerning the process of communication

3.1 INTRODUCTION

The theoretical approaches discussed in this chapter consider communication from a technical point of view. Communication is described as a process of transmission and exchange of information vital to the operation of clearly distinguishable systems. The successful processing and exchange of information is emphasised and an attempt is made to delimit factors which cause "noise" and thereby endanger the successful operation and maintenance of systems.

Although these approaches are applied to "systems", they are focused on the internal operation of systems, rather than the structure of interrelated parts of systems. In fact, the focus on the process of communication within (and between) systems emphasises the need for *structuring* systems to ensure their smooth functioning. Communication systems ultimately consist of human beings, but in this view their significance for the system derives only from their positions in the process of transmission and exchange of information.

Theoretical approaches in this group originated in fields such as mathematics, engineering, biology and physiology. They became popular in communication studies at the time when suitable approaches had to be found for this new field of study. Even today some "technical" approaches are used in the study of communication, since it is maintained that human communication systems operate according to the same principles as organisms and machines. This argument is based on the viewpoint that universal principles apply to all phenomena that, regardless of their specific nature, are capable of being conceptualised as systems. However, it should be emphasised that not all "system approaches" represent the technical view of communication explicated by the approaches covered in this chapter. Functionalism (see Chapter 2, Section 2.2) is a case in point.

A well-known approach in this category is the mathematical information theory, which is normally traced to C.E. Shannon and W. Weaver. In investigating the process of communication between a "source" and a "destination" in a telephone conversation, these authors emphasise the coding and decoding of the message, as well as the possibility that noise may interfere with the successful transmission and reception of the message.

Several varieties of information theory emerged from the foundations laid by Shannon and Weaver. In the field of communication examples include the semantic theory of information and the statistical theory of communication. Information theory has been applied, for example, in the study of political speeches and organisational patterns. In general, modern information theory emphasises that information flows within systems must be investigated, assessed and related to other features of the systems under investigation so as to highlight their operation and to identify possible sources of malfunctioning. The measurement of the quantity of information conveyed in any message is also emphasised (McQuail 1975: 38).

Related to information theory, but perhaps more widely and generally applied in the field of human communication, are cybernetics and general system theory. The following sections briefly outline these approaches and offer a critical assessment of their value in the study of communication.

3.2 CYBERNETICS

This approach, which deals with self-regulation and control of systems, is normally traced to the American mathematician, Norbert Wiener, who derived the term "cybernetics" from a Greek word which refers to the art of steering. However, cybernetic concepts derive from the fields of physiology and engineering as well.

The approach of cybernetics is based on the assumption that systems operate and ensure their survival by counteracting chaos. "Order" is reflected in a state of balance or homeostasis, a notion parallel to the functionalist concept of "equilibrium" (see Chapter 2, Section 2.2.2). Homeostasis is maintained through the operation of a control mechanism, namely the feedback of information concerning the condition of the system. Cybernetics is particularly concerned with the nature of feedback, the "loops" through which it takes place, and its relation to changes in the environment of the system. By acting on feedback information, the system adjusts and readjusts so as to maintain itself in a state of order. This argument implies that the condition of the system is assessed with reference to a norm which defines the "desirable" condition of the system and allows for a certain degree of variation.

Traditionally, negative feedback, that is, information which shows how the system deviates from the norm, was emphasised. By reducing deviation from the norm, negative feedback serves to maintain the status quo. Later developments of cybernetics introduced the possibility of change through positive feedback, that is, information that confirms deviation from the norm and incorporates the notion of an "open" system, oriented towards growth.

Since cybernetics is primarily concerned with the regulatory aspect of system operation, it is often coupled with a more comprehensive approach, namely general system theory. In fact, the latter incorporates the notion of self-regulation through feedback in its view of systems.

3.3 GENERAL SYSTEM THEORY

This approach, which offers the most complete description of communication from a "process" point of view, originated in the work of the biologist L. von Bertalanffy and was later extended to cover all possible systems.

General system theory describes a system as a whole which consists of several interrelated subsystems. The system has characteristics of its own which do not derive from the characteristics of any of its constituent parts. A system may be clearly distinguished from its environment, but maintains important relationships with it in that it receives inputs from the environment and provides outputs to the environment. Since information is the crucial input-output in the system, information channels within and between systems are emphasised. This view presents communication as a circular, rather than linear, process and shows that the system is open, rather than closed.

Systems are goal-oriented and self-maintaining and operate, through feedback, within margins which set the norms for their proper functioning. Feedback derives from output, since the latter illuminates the condition of the system. Input, in turn, reflects system reaction to output, for example adjustments and re-adjustments which keep the system within permissible margins. Basic to the operation of the system is the need to maintain itself in a state of balance. This necessitates control and self-regulation.

The above assumptions correspond with several functionalist assumptions (see Chapter 2, Section 2.2.2). However, the latter place less emphasis on information flow and information channels and more emphasis on the mutual relationships between the constituent parts of the system in general. In addition, general system theory emphasises two important system features which are not particularly emphasised by functionalism. First, the sub-systems of any system are hierarchically arranged in relation to one another (Fauconnier 1985: 100) and, second, the desired state of a system may be accomplished in various ways and from various starting-points, a system feature described as equifinality (Little-john 1983: 32).

In relation to human communication, general system theory has been applied to settings such as organisations and small groups. It is sometimes used for studying interpersonal communication in dyads. Particularly in the first two settings, information concerning the task at hand and/or the human relationships involved to accomplish the task is essential to efficient performance.

3.4 CRITICAL ASSESSMENT

Approaches which view communication as a "technical" process that flows between interrelated parts of a system or between different systems, highlight a certain kind of communication and offer insight into its nature. However, seen from the perspective of the complex and multi-faceted nature of human communication, such approaches offer a limited view indeed. All communication is not geared to efficiency, nor is all communication concerned with the transmission and exchange of information. The technical view of communication oversimplifies the process of communication even in cases where it may be applied, a shortcoming which derives from the assumption that the same general principles apply to all phenomena that, regardless of their nature, may be conceived of as systems.

Seen from the point of view of communication as a process within a system and between systems, general system theory and cybernetics illuminate the nature of interrelationships within and between systems, highlight the effects that interaction between constituent parts of a system may have for the operation of that system and describe the emergence of organisational patterns in systems. On the basis of this view, insight may be gained into matters that influence the effective operation and maintenance of systems, enhance efficiency in the accomplishment of tasks or cause malfunctioning in systems. However, the notion of "open systems oriented towards growth" fails to account for real and fundamental change in systems. The very assumption of homeostasis precludes the possibility of such change because, by upsetting their internal balance, upheavals threaten the survival of systems. General system theory and cybernetics share this shortcoming with functionalism (see Chapter 2, Section 2.2.2). Like functionalism, their general and abstract view of systems and the principles through which they operate, offers no insight into the peculiar characteristics of a particular system. Not only does this detached view fail to inform us about real life; its concern for the maintenance of balance supports the status quo of systems, regardless of the human consequences that their operation may have.

Finally, exponents of general system theory and cybernetics fail to realise that one of the most important sources of "malfunctioning" in a system is precisely the actions of human beings *as human beings*. This is most clearly illustrated in interpersonal communication, that form of communication which enables participants to express their individuality and to participate in an exchange of opinions with their partners. Such conduct simply cannot be accommodated in a system view that disregards the distinctive human nature of communication and depicts communicating human beings as processing units!

3.5 SUMMARY

In this chapter theoretical approaches were introduced which view communication as a process of information flow within and between systems and stress the technical aspects of such communication. Cybernetics and general system theory served to illustrate this kind of approach. Some contributions and limitations of their technical view were discussed as well. The next chapter deals with approaches to the dynamics of communication.

Chapter 4

Theoretical approaches concerning the dynamics of communication

4.1 INTRODUCTION

Theoretical approaches in this group try to capture the nature and essence of communication by focusing on its distinctive human nature. Since only the human being is capable of attributing meaning, communication basically involves the constitution and exchange of meaning between participants. This dynamic, ever-evolving process is based on intersubjectivity, which allows for shared meaning, as well as new meaning which may arise from the encounter itself.

Some approaches in this category emphasise the process whereby meaning becomes shared by participants and/or the way in which existing or new meaning structures communication, while other approaches are concerned rather with the appropriation of meaning by individual participants.

Since several theoretical approaches belong to this category and new ones are still being introduced, in this monograph only four well-known examples are examined, namely symbolic interactionism, phenomenology, existentialism and semiology. In the subsequent discussion each approach is delimited and illustrated with reference to a representative theory. The critical assessment of individual theories offers insight into the communicological value of the approaches which they represent.

4.2 SYMBOLIC INTERACTIONISM

4.2.1 Introduction

Symbolic interactionism, which started developing in North America towards the end of the nineteenth century, is a well-known social scientific approach. Its vitality is illustrated by the fact that its area of study is still expanding, while new ways of approaching it are being explored. In the field of communication studies this approach shows great variety and it is not always clearly distinguished from phenomenology (see Section 4.3 below).

Generally speaking, symbolic interactionism is concerned with the process whereby meaning is constituted and becomes shared by participants in a communication encounter. It stresses the structuring influence exerted on the evolving process of communication by patterns of shared meaning. Meaning is embodied in symbols, such as linguistic symbols, which evoke the same meaning in all participants, thereby structuring their encounter and giving it the character of a symbolic interaction.

Symbolic interactionism regards the ability to attribute meaning to events and experiences as a distinctive human trait and maintains that it goes hand in hand with self-consciousness. Only self-conscious human beings are capable of becoming conscious of other human beings and of adopting the viewpoint of other participants in looking at themselves and the world.

Although this approach maintains that communication is dependent on shared meaning which enables participants to understand one another, it is acknowledged that new meaning may arise from a communication encounter. Recent varieties of the approach even emphasise that shared meaning is the result of a process of negotiation between participants. Negotiation implies tension between individual attribution of meaning and the acceptance of patterns of meaning which have been learnt through social experience. A more detailed discussion of symbolic interactionism is provided by Jansen (1989: 28-47).

For the purposes of this discussion Goffman's dramaturgical theory serves to illustrate the approach of symbolic interactionism.

4.2.2 Goffman's theory

Erving Goffman (1922-1982) was a Canadian-born sociologist whose interest in face-to-face communication in various public and institutional settings makes this theory relevant to several disciplines. Although particularly applicable to interpersonal communication in small groups, some of his assumptions and concepts apply equally to mass communication.

Depending on the focus of the investigation, Goffman's life-work may be divided into different periods. His earlier publications, notably his first book, *The presentation of self in everyday life* (1975), first published in 1959, provide evidence of symbolic interactionist reasoning.

4.2.2.1 A dramaturgical view of communication

Goffman investigates the process whereby meaning is created and becomes shared by participants. He examines this social construction of reality, which he regards as an orderly and deliberately planned process, by studying the parts (roles) which communicating human beings play vis-à-vis one another. Roleplay involves socially acquired and established patterns of behaviour. Since all participants are familiar with the requirements for available roles, they tend to perform the same roles in similar ways, thereby ensuring a stable pattern of behaviour which serves to structure the process of communication and helps to maintain society. Participants are thus known to each other not by their personal characteristics, but by the roles they play.

However, the social self thus portrayed hardly ever entirely coincides with the personal self of participants. In addition, different situations require an accent on different aspects of the social self. Hence communication is inherently problematic and reflects constant tension between social requirements and the need for self-expression.

Goffman is particularly interested in the techniques which participants use to produce, sustain and safeguard social roleplay. He maintains that real life actors and stage actors use the same techniques to present themselves to other people. Hence he uses metaphors from the theatre to explain communication encounters.

Following from his dramaturgical point of departure, Goffman describes a communication encounter as a performance by a team in front of an audience. A team consists of a number of participants who cooperate, for the duration of the encounter, in staging a performance. Since participants continuously take part in different encounters, "team" and "audience" do not denote permanent positions, but must be seen in relation to the specific setting or situation under consideration.

Role prescriptions derive from a shared set of culturally defined meanings and symbols which Goffman calls the ritual code. While the ritual code defines acceptable behaviour in general for a particular society, different roles specify acceptable conduct with reference to specific situations or settings.

Given his emphasis on the social self, Goffman is interested in the type of person represented by a particular kind of role. In theatrical terms we are here dealing with a character that represents the pattern of conduct required by the situation. A character presents a front, a concept that describes for Goffman a fixed and general aspect of an individual person's performance which serves to define the situation for observers of the performance (Goffman 1975: 32). Associated with front are matters such as the physical setting in which the performance takes place and the personal appearance and manner of the performer. Since the performer's real identity is hidden behind the front which he/she presents, one may say that a character wears a mask that suits the requirements of the situation.

To ensure the success of the performance performers must appear credible. If they do not convince the audience that they truly are the characters they play, the audience may regard the performance as false and it may fail to achieve its purpose. Thus Goffman accentuates the need for performers to project a correct definition of the situation, including a definition of the characters involved, at the outset of the performance.

The required information is conveyed through deliberately created impressions (impressions given). To ensure success, such impressions must be sustained throughout the performance. This process of impression management, which is for Goffman the essence of the social construction of reality, involves deliberately emphasising some facts, while playing down others.

Impressions may be created verbally and/or nonverbally. Especially the latter may give the show away by unintentionally disclosing information concerning the personality of the role-player. It is thus imperative that a performance be safeguarded against impressions "given off" and Goffman describes two kinds of techniques which may be used for this purpose (Goffman 1975: 207). Defensive measures are used by performers to save their show. For instance, loyalty to the team prevents its members from becoming so involved with the audience that they disclose the consequences which the show may have for them to the audience. Protective measures, in contrast, are used by the audience and by outsiders to help performers save the show. An audience member may, for example, tactfully announce his/her arrival by giving a sign, such as a cough, to remind performers that they should guard their behaviour.

Ultimately the success of a performance depends on control of discrepant roles, of which several kinds may be distinguished. The informer, for instance, pretends to be a member of the team in order to obtain destructive information, which is then openly or secretly conveyed to the audience (Goffman 1975: 145).

Goffman emphasises the fragility of construed performances and the need for performers to "repair" a discredited performance. He shows that even the most carefully planned performance runs the risk of failing to convince the audience because, even when all precautions have been taken, the personal self of performers is not entirely suppressed. By making (unintentional) mistakes performers "act out of character" and reveal a personal self which usually contradicts the self they are required to play.

Given the fact that performers play different roles and that it requires constant effort on their part to sustain a construed performance, performers need to relax their roleplay from time to time and to prepare for the next performance. While a performance is given on the frontstage, the impressions deliberately created for this purpose are knowingly contradicted as a matter of course on the backstage (Goffman 1975: 114). Backstage behaviour involves acknowledging one's own individuality and that of other members of the team and it is characterised by familiarity shown in behaviour such as reciprocal first-naming, informal remarks and the use of dialects. As they act out different roles in different communication encounters and settings in modern society, performers continuously move from front to backstage and vice versa.

4.2.2.2 Critical assessment

Goffman's account of a communication encounter describes the unfolding of the process whereby reality is socially constructed. By focusing on roleplay he reveals patterns of shared meaning which constitute the foundation of communication encounters and structure participants' behaviour towards one another. Seen from a slightly different perspective, Goffman's focus on the roles people play during communication encounters offers a structural view of the phenomenon of communication. To study the constituent parts of a phenomenon and their mutual relationships is an important way of gaining access to the phenomenon, but of course emphasises only an aspect of the phenomenon.

Although no one would deny the social foundation of communication encounters and the indispensable role of communication in maintaining society, Goffman tends to overemphasise the social dimension of communication. He does acknowledge the need for retaining individuality, but he presents the latter as largely problematic. Failure to suppress the real self interferes with a performer's credibility and endangers the success of a performance.

Goffman's view of communication is particularly applicable to face-to-face communication in small group and institutional settings. But his viewpoint concerning a performance by a character, rather than by an individual person, captures the essence of mass communication as well. Thus his theory illuminates some of the settings in which communication encounters take place and shows that all face-to-face communication is not purely spontaneous, but may be specifically planned and staged.

In conjunction with his use of theatre language, Goffman's representation of communication from a social viewpoint offers a good description of the nature of much of the daily communication in modern society. The demands of modern life, coupled with the variety of roles that a single person must be able to play, simply make it impossible for human beings to become personally involved in all communication encounters. Roleplay thus enables individual persons to deal with different and, at times even contradictory, demands and expectations.

In accordance with symbolic interactionist reasoning, Goffman shows how participants, as self-conscious beings, adopt each other's perspective in looking at themselves, others and the world and how they determine what construed performances mean and what viewpoint they represent. Although his use of metaphors from the theatre enables him to highlight some salient points in this connection, most of his concepts are abstract and do not easily lend themselves to application in real life examples of communication.

Finally, by describing the nature of a performance and highlighting the precautions which should be taken to ensure success, Goffman offers performers in public and institutional settings criteria for assessing and improving their own performance.

4.3 PHENOMENOLOGY

4.3.1 Introduction

Phenomenology originated in the work of the German philosopher, Edmund Husserl (1859-1938), and was only later extended to the field of social scientific inquiry. In communication studies its contribution has not yet been fully explored. Phenomenology is included in this monograph since it offers an interesting new way of looking at communication and examining its ever-evolving character.

Phenomenology starts from the premise that human beings live in a world of meaning which exists over and above their social circumstances and the physical world. The construction of this "life-world" (lebenswelt) comprises an ever-evolving communication process in which human beings participate intersubjectively. Communication not only confirms or reconstitutes some existing meanings; it gives rise to new meanings as well.

Attribution of meaning requires self-conscious human beings. By distancing themselves from the world, human beings adopt a new vantage point for attributing meaning to the world. Since the world can never be experienced as a whole at any moment, the constitution of meaning is constantly done from several vantage points, thus making communication a dynamic, ever-changing process.

Phenomenology focuses on the structure of the "life-world" which consists of those patterns of taken-for-granted meaning that underlie social reality. By enabling participants to categorise events and objects according to their "typical" features, such "root" meanings serve as a frame of reference for determining suitable courses of action in a variety of situations. A more detailed discussion of phenomenology appears in Jansen (1989: 48-63).

To illustrate the approach for the purposes of this monograph, the most influential phenomenological theory in the social sciences, namely Schutz's theory of the life-world, is discussed and critically assessed.

4.3.2 Schutz's theory

The Austrian philosopher and sociologist, Alfred Schutz (1899-1959), tried to make the philosophical approach of phenomenology accessible to the social sciences by blending insights from Husserl with views of the German sociologist, Max Weber (1864-1920). Significant influences in his theory derive from pragmatists and early representatives of symbolic interactionism as well.

Schutz's *The phenomenology of the social world* (1967), first published in German in 1932, laid the foundations for his theory and he explored several aspects of the life-world in his later writings. Since he never completed his project, his communicologically relevant investigations do not represent a complete and coherent picture. The subsequent discussion highlights his most important views concerning the structure of the life-world, while brief reference is made to his analysis of face-to-face and indirect communication. Some critical remarks concerning his contribution are offered as well.

4.3.2.1 The "life-world" and the phenomenon of communication

Schutz is concerned with the world of everyday life that we simply take for granted. This world, which constitutes reality for us, consists of shared commonsense knowledge and taken-for-granted interpretations concerning our daily existence. As a life-world of meaning it is continuously constructed and exists over and above the physical and social world to enable us to interpret our experiences meaningfully. Schutz is mainly concerned with how people come to share a common world and how they interpret their daily experiences so that they mutually understand each other in communication.

In the world of everyday life we operate through the natural attitude. We simply assume that "the world" is the same for all of us and that we all act in it according to the same taken-for-granted knowledge. Likewise, we take the existence of others and our communication with them for granted. For Schutz the natural attitude is a naïve and unquestioned belief in the existence of a shared world and it acts as a stance towards the world, providing us with a basis for interpreting it (Schutz 1970: 320).

At any moment of our lives we occupy a biographically determined position. Not only are our actions influenced by the opportunities and limits of the situations in which we act; they are shaped by our personal history that includes all our previous experiences. Thus two people subjectively experience the same situation differently and express themselves in slightly different terms.

Previous experiences are organised in the form of a stock of knowledge at hand, that is, a common interpretative scheme with reference to which we interpret our past and present experiences and determine our anticipations of things to come (Schutz 1970: 74). In short, we approach the world and orientate ourselves in it with reference to recipes for action, rules of conduct and conceptions of appropriate courses of action which we have acquired through social experience. In turn, the stock of knowledge at hand is arranged into different layers or zones of relevance which determine what is important for an individual human being in a particular situation and at a given time.

The stock of knowledge at hand does not constitute an integrated system, but is constantly in flux. However, as long as contradictory elements are not brought to bear on the same situation, the incoherence of the stock of knowledge is unproblematic (Wagner in Schutz 1970: 16). This argument follows from Schutz's conception of the human being as a "pragmatic" being who acts in particular situations according to his/her interests and involvements at the time.

Schutz emphasises the social nature and prestructured character of the world of everyday life. The greater part of our knowledge of the world is socially derived and is not created by any individual person as such. However, we experience this world intersubjectively (Schutz 1970: 73), that is, each individual person determines the significance of shared meaning for his/her own life by looking at the world of everyday life from his/her own vantage point.

Schutz is particularly interested in the structure of the life-world, that is, in those constructions of reality which are prevalent at a given time. The concept of typification is crucial to his argument. He maintains that our presupposition of a shared world enables us to place people, events, objects and the like into different classes on the basis of common or "typical" features. Typifications enable human beings to find their bearings in the world, to recognise what is relevant in particular situations and to solve practical problems (Wagner in Schutz 1970: 24-25).

In the final analysis culture is the source of meaning. Individuals who share the same culture share the same worldview and believe that they use the same expressions to apply it. In this context Schutz pays special attention to language, the vocabulary and syntax of which he regards as a typifying medium par excellence for transmitting shared knowledge (Schutz 1970: 96). He is also known for his analysis of marks, indications, signs and symbols by which people express and make themselves understandable to others.

The intersubjective world may best be investigated in "direct communication". This basic form of communication involves a face-to-face encounter of human beings who share the same space at a given time and who operate through a common system of typifications. When participants become aware of and intentionally turn towards each other, they enter into a "we-relationship". This relationship, which involves a simultaneous and reciprocal grasping of the other person, makes it possible for participants to experience the social world as "our" world (Natanson in Schutz 1962: xxxiii). The common lived experience of the world in the we-relationship is the basic source of intersubjectivity.

In direct communication partners experience each other as "thou" (you); not only does this imply that they experience each other as persons; they recognise each other as someone like themselves. However, partners do not become alike in direct communication; nor do they enter into each other's lived experience. Schutz maintains that in an immediate, direct way each partner knows only a facet of the personal self of his/her partner; but indirectly partners know a lot about each other, since typifications enable them to determine those characteristics that show what kind of person they are dealing with. This viewpoint challenges the notion, cherished by some critics of mass communication, that "the whole person" is involved in face-to-face communication. Schutz shows that, even in this form of communication, individuals determine their own role and those of other participants by applying socially accepted typifications.

The second form of communication distinguished by Schutz is "indirect" communication. Direct and indirect communication should not be seen as pure types. Schutz places communication encounters on a continuum. As one moves away from face-to-face communication, the personal impact of partners is reduced. In the most extreme case, indirect communication involves communication between types of persons who have very little, if any, physical contact with one another (Schutz 1976: 41). Thus indirect communication involves a "they orientation" among participants.

Schutz illustrates the domain of indirect communication with reference to contemporaries. Although they may have had direct contact in the past and although they are aware of the existence of others who live at the same time, contemporaries are never present to one another as recognisable individual persons. They are experienced and treated through typification, for they are relevant to one another only as typical performers of typical roles (Schutz 1976: 42).

Although Schutz does not refer to mass communication as such, his description of indirect communication captures the essence of mass communication. In its construction of reality mass communication pre-eminently employs a process of typification. As individual persons, participants remain anonymous. They only experience one another as role-players or types which are identified through and treated on the basis of known characteristics.

4.3.2.2 Critical assessment

Schutz is widely recognised, not only as an important twentieth-century philosopher and phenomenologist, but as the person who laid firm foundations for investigating those structures of the social world which enable us to interpret our experiences meaningfully and to understand each other. His treatment of intersubjectivity and typification is particularly important. Not only does he show how and why participants in communication encounters share a common world and yet remain individual persons. He views the patterns of self-evident and taken-for-granted meaning that constitute reality from the point of view of communicating human beings and shows how the process of communication operates in the social construction of reality.

Schutz's description of direct and indirect communication offers insight into the nature and characteristics of face-to-face (interpersonal) and mass communication respectively. His view that face-to-face communication is the basic source of intersubjectivity highlights the need for this form of communication, however complex modern society may become. Unlike those critics of mass communication who tend to regard face-to-face and mass communication as polar types, Schutz shows that they cannot be separated in such a way, since a process of typification is basic to both. The difference between these forms of communication derives rather from the role and significance of typification in each case. In addition, Schutz accentuates the need for both forms of communication in modern society.

Two matters in particular limit Schutz's contribution to the study of communication. First, he approaches the world of everyday life from a sociological viewpoint. This implies not only that he shows a predominant interest in the social dimension of intersubjectivity, but that not all his concepts lend themselves to communicological application. Second, the piecemeal character of his mature writings makes it difficult to fully grasp his views. His treatment of language, indications, signs, marks and symbols is a case in point.

4.4 EXISTENTIALISM

4.4.1 Introduction

Existentialism is a major trend in Western thought. Although it derives from the philosophy of Søren Kierkegaard, several varieties may be distinguished in its development and current application. For the purposes of this monograph Kierkegaard, Buber and Ortega y Gasset are grouped together on the basis of the assumptions outlined below.

Existentialism is concerned with the quality of human existence. By stressing individual appropriation of shared meaning, this approach highlights the crucial role of the individual human being in determining the quality of his/her own existence.

The distinctive mark of authentic existence is self-expression and self-actualisation. For existentialists communication is a mode of existence through which each and every human being may actualise him/herself. In the final analysis, the quality of human existence is revealed in the forms of communication characteristically adopted by human beings.

For authentic self-actualisation to take place, communication must allow for individual participation in appropriation of meaning, individual self-expression and the acknowledgement of the personal self of other participants. Lack of self-actualisation is characterised by forms of communication which reveal little, if any, self-awareness, awareness of other persons and self-expression. Chapter 6 examines Kierkegaard, Buber and Ortega's views concerning the existential consequences of inauthentic communication.

Existentialists emphasise the individual person's freedom in choosing his/her mode of self-expression, as well as his/her responsibility for the choice and its existential consequences.

The short discussion of Kierkegaard's assumptions concerning communication (see Chapter 2, Section 2.3.2.1) offers insight into the existentialist view, but for the purposes of this discussion Buber's dialogical theory is regarded as a representative example. Buber describes authentic communication and self-actualisation by highlighting the evolving relationship between participants in a communication encounter. What happens *between* participants during communication determines the existential significance of the encounter.

4.4.2 Buber's theory

Martin Buber (1878-1965) was a German Jewish philosopher, journalist and author, well-known for his views on dialogue and the contribution he made to the understanding of religious experience, both in Christian and Jewish theology. The relationship between man and God is a theme that underlies all of Buber's thinking and is inherent in his description of the relationships between people as well as his views on society and community. He was professor of Jewish studies and ethics at Frankfurt University and editor of several publications. The rise of Nazism resulted in his emigration to Palestine in 1938, where he became professor of social philosophy at the Hebrew University in Jerusalem. His life-long interest in Zionism and the attempts he made to initiate dialogue between Jews and Arabs led to his co-leadership of the Yihud Movement which was directed at the creation of a bi-national state in Israel. The discussion that follows concerns Buber's theory of dialogue, which represents an existential approach to communication and is based on *I and Thou* (1970), first published in German in 1923, *Between man and man* (1964) and *The knowledge of man* (1965). His critique of communication in modern society is discussed in Chapter 6, Section 6.3.2.

4.4.2.1 Buber's anthropological assumptions

Buber sees the world and the human being's relationship to the world in terms of a twofold principle of polar opposites. For Buber (1964) the human being is able to enter into living relationships with the world. He explains the nature of these relationships in terms of two basic movements from which the twofold principle of human life is derived — distance and relation. In the first movement the individual distances him/herself from the world as a whole, separating him/herself from other people and objects. In the second movement he/she establishes a relationship with them. The importance of these relationships is that "distance provides the human situation, relation provides man's becoming in that situation" (Buber 1965: 64). Entering into relation, which means entering into communication, is the act by which people constitute themselves as human, and is an act which must be continually repeated in every situation.

Buber is concerned with authentic human existence. The fundamental fact of existence in his theory is that people are communicating beings. Communication is the only way in which people gain knowledge of themselves and fulfil themselves as human beings. Their access to being is thus through their communication relationships. Buber (1970: 62) expresses this as "all real living is meeting". Relationship means mutual affirmation, co-operation and genuine dialogue. Entering into relationship creates what Buber (1964: 244) calls "the sphere of the between". In the sphere of the between people affirm each other, each becoming a self with the other. The growth of the self thus depends not only on the individual's relationship to him/herself, but on the nature of his/her relationships to other people. For this reason, Buber does not concentrate on either the individual or the group in communication, but on what takes place *between* them. Buber (1970) explains the nature of the relationships between people by describing two communication encounters, I-you and I-it. Each of these word-pairs creates and reveals a mode of existence.

4.4.2.2 *Communication relationships*

I-you and I-it are two word-pairs which describe the relationship between the partners in communication. The "I" of the person comes into being in the act of speaking one or other of these word-pairs. But the "I" that speaks is different in each case and the relationship that is established is different. The attitude and intentions of the partners differ in the two ways of communicating.

I-you is the primary word of relationship. The "I" reaches out to the "you" with his/her whole being and the you responds with his/her whole being. They approach each other with mutual respect, sincerity and honesty, and the intention to become subjectively involved in a reciprocal relationship. This is the true state of dialogue — the relationship between two equal subjects. The participants communicate from lived experience and each reveals the being that he/she is, not the image of him/herself that he/she would like the other to have. In addition to revealing him/herself as he/she is, the "I" also accepts the other as the unique individual that he/she is. He/she is present to the other in the sense that he/she listens attentively to what the other wishes to express and tries to understand his/her point of view. I-you is thus the expression of an authentic mode of existence.

I-it is the expression of an inauthentic mode of existence. I-it is the primary word of experiencing and using in which the "I" regards the other as an "it", an object. It is not a true relationship in that it takes place within the individual and not between him/herself and another. It is a state of monologue in which the "I" cannot reach out to the other — he/she can neither listen attentively nor respond. Words which Buber (1970) uses to characterise the I-it relationship include, among others: domination, self-centredness, pretence, exploitation, and manipulation. I-it is not a relationship of mutual trust, openness and reciprocity, but one in which the "I" uses and manipulates the other as an instrument to achieve his/her own ends.

It is important to be aware that I-you and I-it are word-pairs; in each pair, neither word has an independent existence. The "I" can never be spoken alone because the process of becoming only takes place in relationship with another person. Buber suggests that in dialogue a space opens up between people. This is the interhuman realm, the "between" where you and I become the self that we are. Two ways of becoming are manifested in the sphere of the between: "being" and "seeming". Being proceeds from what one really is, while seeming results from what one wishes to seem. Being facilitates the development of a we-relationship. The we-relationship is an authentic being-with-others (an I-you relationship) in which the "I" reveals him/herself as he/she is and affirms the other as the person that he/she is. Seeming is an inauthentic being-with-others (an I-it relationship). The "I" does not reveal his/her authentic self, nor does he/she express his/her true self in the communication encounter with the other. He/she is concerned only with the impression of him/herself that he/she wants the other to have. Because mutual participation and involvement between the participants is lacking, there is no affirmation of the other and no growth of the self. Buber (1965) argues that the problem of modern existence, the deteriorating relationships between people, lies in the sphere of the between, in the duality of being and seeming. (See Chapter 6, Section 6.3.2 for Buber's views on this topic.)

Buber does not suggest that the we-relationship is easily established or that the meaning of existence is easily found. Meaning is, however, always open and waiting to be realised. Buber (1964) uses the metaphor of a "narrow ridge" to describe the tenuous and uncertain nature of the we-relationship. Buber says that you and I meet on a narrow ridge between the waves, where the only certainty is that of encounter and undiscovered truth. You and I both remain our true selves — individuals — but together, we strive for the truth. The meaning of human existence is disclosed in the dialogue that unfolds between us.

Buber acknowledges that the I-you relationship cannot be sustained indefinitely. In order to survive in the modern world I-it relationships are necessary, but he emphasises that I-it relationships should not be allowed to overtake one's life; I-it relationships should always remain subordinate to I-you relationships. This implies that people do not choose one mode of existence to the exclusion of the other. Depending on the particular situation, they oscillate between being and seeming. One can thus distinguish between people who (for the most part) are, and those who mostly seem. True existence, the basis for dialogical encounter, requires that the individual overcomes the tendency towards adopting a seeming mode of existence and manifests his/her true self.

Buber (1970) describes a third relationship, the I-eternal-you. For Buber, as for many other existentialist philosophers, an authentic existence assumes a relationship with a divine being, the "eternal-you". In Buber's theory the "eternal-you" is the God of the Old Testament. The meeting with the "eternal-you" is the highest form of relationship. God can only be encountered as a "you", never as an "it". This is because God is not an object of discourse, knowledge or experience, thus the relationship cannot be acquired as a possession; it must be lived. The only way to realise a relationship with God is to address him and be addressed by him, in the present, the here-and-now. God is present in all things, and the possibility of establishing a relationship with him is ever present. The individual takes the decisive step, turns his/her back on the it-world, abandons his/her pursuit of false values, and opens him/herself to God.

The emphasis in Buber's theory of dialogue is not on the "eternal-you", but on "you". Buber is concerned with the individual's relationship to other people, not with the nature of his/her religion. The importance of the "eternal-you" relationship is that it underlies and consummates all authentic interhuman relationships. It is only in the encounter with God that people become fully human. Only the person who enters into an I-eternal-you relationship can truly say "you" to other people, and all I-you relationships meet in the "eternal-you".

4.4.2.3 Critical assessment

Buber's ideas about dialogue and authentic human existence have not only made a contribution to communication studies, but to disciplines such as theology, politics, psychology, art and education. Buber is acknowledged as having made some of the richest religious experience available to Christian theology; he is in fact more widely read and drawn upon by Christianity than by Judaism. (To gain a complete understanding of Buber's contributions to the field of communication, this section should be read in conjunction with Chapter 6, Section 6.3.2 in which his assessment of mass communication is discussed.)

Although Buber does not provide any new perspectives on dialogue, he offers an explicit description of the nature and characteristics of two modes of existence, and examines their meaning in modern life. He makes an important contribution to an understanding of dialogue by drawing attention to the relationship between the partners in communication, a relationship that does not reside within either participant, but without which dialogue cannot exist. The first requirement for a dialogical relationship is an understanding of oneself. That understanding is deepened through the dialogue. Thus, the meaning of the encounter lies not so much in the individual meaning that is created, but the meaning that comes into being when they meet. Buber emphasises that what happens between people in dialogue is responsible for the quality of individual existence. However, his concentration on the participants in communication and the quality of their participation, means that he does not pay a great deal of attention to the role that the medium plays in influencing interpersonal relationships, as well as the social positions of the participants, which can have a detrimental effect on the nature of their relationship.

Buber was not the first author to describe the conditions for dialogic communication, or to explain dialogue as a union of opposites. However, what makes his work particularly interesting is his insistence on two antithetical modes of existence — being and seeming — as the core of dialogue, and the fact that it is the human being's constant struggle between these two contraries that makes true dialogue possible. Buber's insight is particularly relevant to contemporary life-styles as he clarifies that the decision to pursue I-you relationships is in fact the pursuit of freedom — it is a choice against the easy way of adopting societal norms and values and the temptation to exploit others for one's own benefit. He emphasises that ultimately, however, the type of relationship and mode of existence that predominate in each person's life remains the choice and responsibility of the individual him/ herself.

4.5 SEMIOLOGY

4.5.1 Introduction

Semiology is the science of signs. It developed from the philosophy of structuralism which proposes that human behaviour, thus also communication behaviour, is governed by an underlying system of ever-changing cultural and social structures. Semiology is based on the premise that any object or action (that is, any sign) that generates meaning does so by virtue of a system of conventions or rules that governs its use. Semiology thus provides a method for the analysis of the nature of signs and the relationship between signs and the production of meaning. Its field of study includes everything that can be used for communication, from words, images, gestures, dress and hairstyles to more complex sign systems such as music, advertisements, film, television and so on.

The value of semiology for the study of communication is that it makes people aware of the fact that they communicate by means of signs that have fixed or non-fixed meanings, and that communication constantly involves the transmission of meaning or meanings. It differs from the other approaches in this chapter in that it does not focus on the way in which meaning is produced and exchanged between the partners in communication. It is concerned with how messages themselves interact with people to produce meaning. The message is both the object and subject of semiological analysis. Messages are seen as being composed of signs and codes which derive meaning from the culture in which they arise. Semiology studies the relationship between the sign, the message, the users, and the culture.

Semiology developed from the work of the Swiss linguist, Ferdinand de Saussure (1857-1913) and the American philosopher, Charles Peirce (1839-1914). The analytical framework of semiology is adopted from the linguistic model developed by Saussure in his *Course in general linguistics* (1974), first published in 1916. It concentrates on understanding the structured set of relationships within a sign system (such as language) that enables a message to signify meaning independently of the material world.

Peirce focused on the functions rather than the structure of signs. As a philosopher, he was interested in the nature of knowledge and how knowledge is derived from the logical functioning of all signs, not only linguistic signs, that produce meaning in a culture. Peirce's ideas are found in his *Collected works* (1931-1958). Saussure and Peirce's ideas are closely related and together they constitute the foundation of semiology.

Semiology flourished in France in the 1950s and 1960s. An important modern exponent of semiology is the French author and critic Roland Barthes (1915-1980), who extended and enlarged Saussure's original concept of language to include all social practices in society. For the purposes of this discussion, Barthes' most important works are *Elements of semiology* (1967) and *Mythologies* (1972).

To explain how meaning is created, semiology uses a specialised vocabulary to describe signs and how they function. The subsequent discussion focuses on its concepts with reference to the work of Saussure, Peirce and Barthes.

4.5.2 The semiological approach

Saussure inherited the traditional nineteenth-century view that language is constituted of separate units called "words", each of which has a separate "meaning" attached to it, the whole being studied *diachronically* (historically) in terms of observable and recordable changes over time. Saussure argues that a language should be studied in terms of the relationships between its constituent parts as well as *synchronically*, that is, in terms of its current usage. He thus makes a distinction between *langue*, the theoretical system or structure of language, and *parole*, the individual act of communication which the system produces, which we call speech. Saussure maintains that langue, not parole, is the primary object of a science which aims to show how language functions. He is thus not concerned with investigating what people actually say or the real objects which they speak about. He considers how language and its constituent elements (signs) function as a complete system to communicate meaning.

Saussure conceptualises the sign as the union of two elements: the *signifier* and the *signified*. The signifier is the material aspect of the sign: a sound or its written equivalent. The signified is the mental concept or idea which it represents. The sign "tree", for example, is composed of four letters of the alphabet (the signifier) and the image that the sound/written word evokes in our minds (the signified). The object to which the sign refers in reality (the tree that grows in the ground) is the referent. Saussure separates the sign from its referent and concerns himself with the way in which the relationship between signifier and signified communicates meaning.

Saussure argues that the linguistic sign (unlike a drawing, for example), is non-motivated or *arbitrary* in that the signifier relates to the signified by cultural convention. There is no natural association between the signifier "tree" and its signified tree. There is also no natural relationship between the sign and its referent (the tree in reality). Words thus have no meaning in themselves. Instead, a word's meaning derives from its difference from other words in the sign system of language. The signifier "cat", for example, has meaning not in itself, but because it is not cap or cad or bat. Its signified is meaningful because of its difference from dog, pig, cow, and so on.

The arbitrary nature of the sign shows that words do not depend on reality for their meaning, nor is meaning determined by the subjective intention of the user. The linguistic system as a whole produces the meaning. In other words, it is not things that determine the meaning of words; words determine the meaning of things.

Saussure describes two ways in which signs are combined into meaningful systems or codes — *syntagmatic* (horizontal) and *associative* or *paradigmatic* (vertical) relationships. A syntagm is the order or sequence in which signs are combined. "Cap", for example, has meaning only in terms of the sequential relationship between the three letters, c, a, and p. "The cap is blue" is a meaningful sentence only because of the syntagmatic relationship between the four words. A paradigm is a set of signs from which the one to be used is chosen. For example, the words, "pretty" or "attractive" or "handsome", although similar in meaning, are also slightly different. Saussure maintains that the words that have not been chosen in the sequence help to define the meaning of the word which has. The word chosen differentiates the meaning for the user. All messages thus involve selection (from a paradigm) and combination (into a syntagm). The selection and combination of words and sentences comprises a complete language-system.

The importance of Saussure's concept of language and the linguistic sign is that the field of study of semiology can be extended to include non-linguistic systems of communication that are studied *like* a language (e.g. the "languages" of art, colours, photography, film, literature, advertising, dress, and so on). Such a "language" is a specific system of signs with its own laws of functioning. Semiology today is most commonly used to study non-linguistic sign systems.

Peirce was also interested in sign systems and the way in which they function. He did not limit himself to linguistics, but tried to account for every type of sign. According to Peirce a sign is something which stands to somebody in some respect or capacity. In his study of signs, Peirce distinguishes a threefold relationship which is roughly similar to Saussure's signifier, signified and referent. The sign itself (*representatum*), the literal meaning of the object represented (*designatum*), and the mental concept (*interpretent*) which is formed by the user. The interpretent is usually a second sign (e.g. a synonym), which enables the user to interpret and understand the object. Unlike Saussure, Peirce does not separate the sign from its referent (object). He sees the sign, its object, and the users of the sign (including the user's cultural experience) as three points of a triangle. Each is closely related to the other two and can only be understood in terms of the others. To explain how signs signify (stand for something else), Peirce proposes three categories of sign, each of which shows a different relationship between the sign and its object: *icon*, *index* and *symbol*.

An iconic sign (or icon) bears a resemblance to its object in some way; it looks or sounds like it. A photograph is an icon, as is a map, and the diagrams commonly used to denote ladies and gentlemen's cloakrooms. The hissing sound — sss — that we use to denote a snake is a verbal icon; it sounds like its object. An indexical sign (or index) has a direct connection with its object. Thus, smoke is an index of fire, a sneeze is an index of hayfever, a knock on the door is an index of someone's presence. A symbolic sign (or symbol) bears a connection to its object as the result of convention, agreement or rule. The relationship is arbitrary. Words and numbers are symbols; there is no reason why the shape 2 should refer to a pair of objects other than convention or rule in our culture. Similarly, the red cross on an ambulance is a universal symbol, while the owl is a symbol of learning in Western cultures. Arising from Peirce's system is the fact that anything which can be isolated, and then connected with something else and interpreted, can function as a sign.

Peirce's analysis complements the groundwork laid by Saussure in that he categorises the types of signs that exist in society, and explains the way that they function within a cultural context. Pierce's classification lays the foundation for a typology of signs which has been extended from different perspectives in contemporary semiological studies. Modern exponents of Peirce's ideas include the Italian semiologist Umberto Eco, the British scholars C.K. Ogden and I.A. Richards, and the American behavioural philosopher Charles Morris.

Roland Barthes broadens the field of Saussurian semiology by considering not only the relationship between signifier and signified in the construction of meaning, but the relationship between the message (text) and its user. He shows how the socio-cultural background of the user influences the meaning which the text communicates. For Barthes, the construction and interpretation of meaning is interactive and involves a process of negotiation between user and text.

Barthes explains the way in which signs work in terms of two orders of signification. *Denotation* is the first order of signification and refers to the commonsense, obvious relationship between signifier and signified, and between the sign as a whole and its referent in reality. *Connotation* is a second-order signifying system that uses the first (denotative) sign as its signifier, and attaches a different meaning to it. For example, the sign "roses" evokes in our minds a bunch of a particular species of flower (its denotative meaning). But when a bunch of roses is used to signify passion, for example, its meaning is interpreted connotatively. The bunch of roses becomes a signifier of which the signified is passion. The new signifier/signified relationship is a sign on the second level of signification. Its meaning depends on the cultural context in which it is used and the feelings and intentions of its user. In film, for example, the choice of light, focus, black and white or colour film, connotes the photographer's feelings about the denotative object/event that he photographs.

Closely related to connotation is *myth*. A myth, in Barthes' theory, does not refer to classical mythology, but to the cultural and ideological meaning of a sign or message. It is a way of conceptualising and understanding social practices such as masculine/

feminine roles, science, or art. Barthes thinks of myths as a chain of related concepts (signifieds), the meaning of which depends on the meanings that the chain already has in the culture. For example, the Mandela-myth in South African society includes concepts of liberation, equality, armed struggle, and so on. Thus, a photograph of Mandela evokes images that existed before the photograph itself; the photograph activates the chain of concepts that constitute the myth.

Barthes' semiological studies concentrate mainly on the mass communication media, advertising, and popular culture. His work shows that second-order signification is an extremely powerful covert producer of meaning in society where an impression is given that existing reality is universal and natural. Barthes argues that the mass media are the greatest purveyors of mythical meanings in society, and thus of ideology. Every time a sign is used it reinforces the life of its second-order meaning both in the culture and in its user. Barthes' *Mythologies* (1972) is an exercise in unmasking the apparently natural association between signifier and signified in the denotative sign. He shows that the link between the denotative sign and its connotative meaning is not causal, but arbitrary, and is socially determined by the dominant ideas of the society in which it is used.

4.5.3 Critical assessment

Saussure's study of linguistics and the semiological concepts that he introduced have influenced contemporary thinking about people, language and reality. Since the 1960s, the model of language first suggested by Saussure has increasingly been used to analyse and describe the structures, functions and meanings of the underlying sign systems that constitute a variety of social practices which include communication, history, social anthropology, psychology, literature and philosophy.

Semiology provides a systematic method for analysing and understanding how messages are constructed. By concentrating on structural relationships within a sign system such as language, it rejects the possibility that meaning is individually constituted and allows for the rules by which it is culturally produced and shared, to be revealed.

Its emphasis on the cultural context highlights the conventional and arbitrary nature of many of the signs that we encounter in everyday life and which we accept as natural and unchanging. In this respect, semiology is particularly useful for the study of a complex sign system such as television. People tend to believe that what they see on television is the truth. An understanding of semiology can make one aware that visual images do not always have a natural connection with what they stand for, but that meaning is established through social convention.

If signs are conventional, their meanings are subject to change. Seiter (in Allen 1987: 29) points out that the chief drawback of semiology is that it is based on a synchronic and thus static model of the sign, which makes it difficult to explain how changes in meaning are produced by a sign system such as television, often as a justification of the dominant ideas in society. Barthes overcomes this limitation by revealing how connotation and myth can be used to produce new meanings in television (and other mass media) messages. For example, since February 1990, the South African Broadcasting Corporation has made use of second-order signification to communicate a new perception of the African National Congress to South African viewers. Importantly, Barthes' studies make it possible for the *recipient* of mass media messages to gain an understanding of the covert messages that are communicated. Barthes' work also lays the foundation for important recent developments in media and text analysis such as postmodernism and deconstruction.

4.6 SUMMARY

In this chapter four theoretical approaches which view communication as a dynamic, ever-evolving process were introduced. Although symbolic interactionism, phenomenology, existentialism and semiology all explain the dynamics of communication with reference to the constitution and exchange of meaning, each highlights the process from a different viewpoint. A theory representing each approach was discussed and critically assessed. The next two chapters deal with approaches that offer a critical appraisal of the quality or condition of communication.

Chapter 5

Social and cultural critique of communication

5.1 INTRODUCTION

In Chapter 1, Section 1.3.2, approaches to the critical appraisal of communication were divided into two groups. The present chapter deals with social and cultural criticism, while existentialist critique is discussed in Chapter 6. In each case some assumptions concerning communication and the need for assessing its quality are presented, followed by a discussion of well-known representative theories. A critical assessment of the latter offers insight into the contributions and shortcomings of the two approaches in general.

Generally speaking, authors who adopt a social and cultural viewpoint share the following assumptions concerning the nature and quality of communication. Communication is embedded in society and its nature and characteristics are determined by the structural arrangements and conditions obtaining in a particular society at a given time. Not only the positions of participants in communication, but the nature of their encounter and the quality of their modes of expression, such as culture, are determined thus. Hence critical appraisal of the condition of the phenomenon of communication is inseparably bound up with critical assessment of the kind of society in which communication takes place.

Authors who adopt this viewpoint are specifically concerned with *capitalist* society and investigate particular examples of this kind of society. Their yardstick for assessing capitalist society is an image of a "just" society, for example, a society which offers its members equal opportunities for developing their human potential, participating in decisions concerning matters which affect their lives and creating culture. They argue that capitalist society, in contrast, is usually run by a small minority that wields power in all walks of life. Not only is access to opportunities for participating in the affairs of society controlled by the dominant group but by steering the entire process of communication and controlling cultural production, the ruling minority determines the very content of their subjects' lives. Some authors in this tradition are not so much interested in the structure of capitalist society as such, but concur with the viewpoint that, in capitalist society, people's lives are controlled by a powerful "structure" which sustains and maintains itself through a manipulatory ideology.

Since the quality of communication is dependent on the structure of society, fundamental change in social arrangements, particularly in the power structure of society, is considered the only solution to the problem of human existence in capitalist society. To elicit the co-operation of the ordinary members of society in overthrowing capitalist society, exponents of this approach propose a process of conscientisation.

The remainder of this chapter introduces five well-known authors who highlight different aspects concerning a social and cultural critique of society and its system of (mass) communication.

5.2 GEORGE ORWELL

5.2.1 Introduction

George Orwell is the pseudonym of Eric Arthur Blair (1903-1950), an eminent British writer. During his lifetime he was known for his journalism, essays and book reviews, but he is probably best remembered for two successful novels, Animal Farm (1983), first published in 1945, and Nineteen eighty-four (1984), first published in 1949.

Orwell's writings show a concern with genuine as well as "distorted" communication. The first topic revolves around issues such as "a committed literature" and the role of the writer in society. His views on distorted communication, which are discussed in some detail below, involve a penetrating analysis of human existence and communication under conditions of totalitarian control, a phenomenon which has recently been highlighted by events in Eastern Europe.

To be able to fully appreciate Orwell's views, one should first consider the existential circumstances which provided the impetus for his writing.

The era in which Orwell lived was characterised by struggle, social upheavals, violence and revolutionary movements. For instance, the rise of Stalinism and Fascism replaced democratic political structures with one-party states and introduced increasingly greater control of cultural expression. Orwell was alarmed at the threat which these developments posed to individual freedom and opportunities for self-expression. In addition, the average citizen suffered the disrupting consequences of two world wars and a world-wide economic depression in the thirties. In the late twenties and thirties England, in particular, witnessed widespread poverty and unemployment. Finally, Britain lost her position as mighty empire, a loss which was not easily forgotten by the British.

Orwell's personal experiences also contributed to his growing awareness of the quality of human existence in his day and of the forces responsible for it. Two particularly significant events in this connection were his visit to Northern England to investigate the living conditions of the poor and unemployed and his brief participation in the Spanish Civil War.

His awareness of the existential consequences of the above developments was accompanied by a strong urge to expose the lies and pretences behind seemingly correct behaviour and wise decisions of the rulers. He explains the purpose of his writing as follows in the well-known essay, "Why I write": ". . . to push the world in a certain direction, to alter people's ideas of the kind of society they should strive after" (Orwell 1979: 26).

Orwell values the individual spirit and emphasises the need for cultural expression by autonomous individuals. He is particularly concerned with literature as a mode of expression and proposes a "committed literature" which aims at involving the reader in a process of critical appraisal and responsible action towards improving society and the prevailing mode of existence.

A committed literature requires committed writers with a free outlook and an ability to use language in a simple, yet precise and imaginative way in order to offer an honest account of what they observe. Orwell's "political writing" which, in the final analysis, is a fusion of political and artistic purpose aimed at conscientising his readers (Orwell 1979: 29), is a significant contribution to a committed literature.

The subsequent discussion outlines important aspects of Orwell's critique of communication in totalitarian society, while brief mention is made of the alternative mode of existence which he envisages. Some critical comments concerning his communicological contributions are offered as well.

5.2.2 Orwell's critique of communication

Orwell adopts a social and cultural approach in that he maintains that the mode and quality of communication are decisively influenced by the structure of and prevailing conditions in society. Since society is ultimately a political phenomenon, its nature and structure and the mode of existence adopted by its members are determined by political decisions in the widest sense of the word. Although Orwell highlights totalitarian trends in democratic society as well, he is particularly concerned with totalitarian society and the limitations it imposes on individual thought and expression. He is known especially for his investigation into the manipulative use of distorted language.

Orwell's best description of a totalitarian system appears in *Animal Farm* (1983) and *Nineteen eighty-four* (1984). In the latter, for instance, the small almost all-powerful group of rulers consists of the Inner Party, headed by Big Brother, and the Outer Party, a faction of the Inner Party which has no real power. The Proles constitute a vast majority of subjects. Its access to almost total power enables the Party to determine the entire set of circumstances in which the Proles live, as well as the contents of their world.

The Party devises an elaborate control system to safeguard its position. Agents, such as the Thought Police, are constantly engaged in tracing the slightest sign of resistance to the System. The Party's aim is the total subjugation of the subjects and it does not hesitate to use physical force against dissidents. Distorted language, in the form of *newspeak*, and an advanced mass communication system effectively create a new world for the subjects and control their experience of it.

The mode of existence in totalitarian society is characterised by features such as loss of individual autonomy, the absence of truth and full control by the rulers of all modes of cultural expression. Subjects are confronted with only one way of looking at the world, that way which suits the rulers best. In an attempt to prevent the occurrence of counter-interpretations, literary expression is for instance suppressed. After all, such freedom of thought may introduce avenues for resistance to the regime. Hence, Orwell maintains, a fully-fledged totalitarian society has no literature in the normal sense of the word.

To suppress freedom of expression ultimately means to suppress the truth about the real interests behind the System. Hence strict censorship and the widespread use of propaganda in favour of the rulers are characteristic of totalitarian societies.

Another useful way of producing the desired image of reality which suits the interests of the rulers is to re-interpret history. In *Nineteen eighty four*, for instance, the Ministry of Truth is responsible for falsifying historical records. In this way the image of the Party and its glorious deeds are created and supplant all memories of the past and fill the subjects with expectations about the Party's future achievements. Since control of the past involves control of the future as well, the rulers can easily perpetuate the status quo.

Orwell is particularly known for his analysis of totalitarian control by means of a transformation of language. *Newspeak*, the language described in *Nineteen eighty-four*, offers an extreme example. In *newspeak* language is compressed to remove all possible shades of meaning implied in words. The simple notion which is substituted for the original meaning(s) of a word eliminates all evaluative and critical assessment which may stimulate individual thought and expression. In conjunction with means such as the re-interpretation of history, *newspeak* creates a false consciousness which ensures that subjects willingly surrender themselves to the System.

It should be noted in passing that Orwell also investigates ways in which distorted language and particular styles of writing may serve to introduce a measure of totalitarian control into democratic societies. In several essays Orwell (1979; 1980) shows how the use of conventional rhetorical form, for instance, enforces a particular pattern of thinking which eliminates individual appro-

priation of meaning and makes the reader susceptible to manipulation.

Orwell gives a clear account of the process whereby totalitarian
control is established and highlights the crucial role of communication in this process. *Animal Farm* offers a good illustration. After
having rid themselves of the yoke of oppression by the farmer, the
animals experience true equality and are united by the ideology of
Animalism. However, some animals soon become "more equal
than others" and their access to privileges gives rise to misuse of
power and total control over the process of communication. The
ensuing power struggle is won by Napoleon and under his reign of
terror the animals are more oppressed than ever before.

Orwell's belief in individual autonomy and the need for freedom
of expression is reflected in his socialistic alternative to totalitar-
ianism. In his opinion a socialist society is a planned society which
serves the interests of the majority and guarantees freedom and
justice for all. He believes that equal opportunities for developing
their human potential will enable the members of society to
improve the quality of their existence. Although he envisages a new
kind of political structure and firmly rejects the Soviet (Stalinist)
system, he does not offer a clear description of a socialist society
and its communication system. Instead, he highlights an underlying socialistic principle which may be embodied in different kinds
of structural arrangements. Given his experience of unjust societies
and his acute awareness of the need to safeguard individual power
of expression, his proposal is an individualistic and uniquely
Orwellian version of socialism.

5.2.3 Critical assessment

Orwell is concerned with the phenomenon of tyranny, irrespective
of the kind of society in which it occurs. He shows what absolute
seizure of power entails, how absolute power may be exercised
(among other ways through the process of communication) and he
highlights the frightening existential consequences of this phenomenon for the lives of ordinary human beings. His investigation
into totalitarian trends in seemingly democratic societies sounds a
warning that appearances may deceive. The significance of his
observations in this connection is accentuated by Mills' critique of

the (American) democratic mass society and its mode of communication (see Section 5.4.2.2 below). Although *Animal Farm* and *Nineteen eighty-four* seem to be aimed at Stalinism, Orwell's *Collected essays* (1979; 1980) prove beyond doubt that he was as critical of Fascism as of Stalinism. This conclusion is borne out by his reactions to the Spanish Civil War.

One of Orwell's most useful contributions is his analysis of the modes of control and manipulation and the process of communication used by totalitarian rulers and his description of the institutionalisation of such control in society. His analysis of language as a means of communication is often regarded as his outstanding contribution to the study of this topic.

Although he deals with the writer, Orwell in fact accentuates the responsibility and need for commitment on the part of the communicator in modern society. He stresses qualities such as honesty and frankness, which mark a genuinely concerned communicator, highlights values which distinguish the committed communicator from the manipulator and offers guidelines as to how recipients may be involved in interpretation. Although the latter contribution is not unique, it is significant since his views apply specifically to modern mass communication.

Orwell's image of a just society is based on the notion of equality, but he does not advocate levelling. Instead, he emphasises the relationship between individuality and creativity, a crucial point often overlooked by authors who advocate the principle of equality. Orwell shows that joint action in the interest of bringing about real change is dependent upon guiding ideas which derive from *individual* involvement in society. However, his socialistic alternative, which accommodates this principle, is vague and difficult to implement. In addition, Orwell offers no guidelines as to how a socialistic society, based on his ideas, may be brought about.

Finally, it should be noted that Orwell, like Mills (see Section 5.4.3 below), is inclined to exaggerate the role of politics in society and in shaping the prevailing mode of existence. However important it may be, all significant decisions and events in modern society and in relation to communication in modern society cannot be reduced to political issues and/or the exercise of political power.

5.3 HERBERT MARCUSE

5.3.1 Introduction

Marcuse (1898-1979) was a German American social philosopher and associate of the Institute for Social Research at Frankfurt University. Hitler's rise to power in 1933 forced the removal of the Institute to New York where it was affiliated to Columbia/ University. When his colleagues went back to Germany in the early 1950s, Marcuse remained in America and taught at the universities of Brandeis and San Diego. His critical views made him the favourite mentor of the student revolutionaries of the 1960s. His well-known publications include *Reason and revolution* (1955), first published in 1941, *Eros and Civilization* (1956) and *One-dimensional man* (1964).

The critical theory of the Frankfurt School is a theory of social transformation which developed as a reaction to Stalinism and Fascism. It is critical of capitalist industrial societies such as the United States. A more detailed discussion of the Frankfurt School is to be found in Jansen (1989: 9-12). Marcuse, together with his colleagues Adorno and Lowenthal, concentrate in particular on the relationship between culture and mass society. They draw on Marx's early writings on cultural criticism which the school believed had been neglected in favour of his economic determinism.

Although concerned with the contamination of traditional "high" culture by the mediocre standards of "mass" culture, the chief concern of the Frankfurt School was that mass culture tends to mute the sources of intellectual opposition which are essential if the prospects of social change are to be realised. These prospects have been severely curtailed in modern society because the consciousness of a need for change among the masses has been eliminated. Their contention was that the apparent political stability which had been achieved in the post-war Western world was the result of ideological indoctrination of the masses by the ruling regime, assisted by the technological developments of the period. Marcuse shared the concern of the Frankfurt School for the liberation of the masses from domination. The subsequent discussion is based mainly on *One-dimensional man* (1964) in which Marcuse shows how the potential of the working classes for effective action has been subverted by creating a pattern of one-dimensional thought and action in society.

5.3.2 Marcuse's critique of mass communication

In essence, Marcuse's criticism of American society is that it is a one-dimensional society. The second, or missing, dimension is the dimension which, in societies of the early nineteenth century, comprised the forces of social, political, cultural and communicological opposition that Marx believed were necessary to bring about the downfall of capitalism and a qualitative transformation in the lives of the masses. Marcuse describes how these forces have been integrated into modern society so that they are rendered ineffectual.

5.3.2.1 Social and political integration

Marcuse maintains that tho prevailing means of social control in advanced industrial societies are technological. Unlike Ellul (see Section 5.6 below), he does not regard technology as an autonomous system, but as an instrument of repression in the hands of the ruling regime. The abundant supply of mass produced goods, for example, is used to sustain the material or false needs which have been predetermined by the interests of a capitalist society, and to which people are conditioned. False needs are thus superimposed on the individual by economic and political interests, and include the needs to relax, to have fun, to behave and consume in accordance with advertisements and to love and hate what others love and hate (Marcuse 1964: 5). The fulfilment of false needs serves to subvert the recognition of real or qualitative needs in the life of the individual. True needs are the needs for nourishment, clothing, and lodging at the attainable level of culture. The problem that Marcuse identifies is that modern man cannot determine true needs, because he is not free. His critical faculty has been contained so that the consciousness of a need for qualitative change in his life is eliminated. This is achieved on a socio-psychological level in the following way (Marcuse 1964: 9-10).

In two-dimensional life, people have an individual consciousness apart from public opinion and behaviour — an inner private space in which each one may become and remain him/herself. In this dimension resides the power of reason or critical thinking.

Today, this private space has been invaded by technological domination. The rising standard of living has blunted critical perception so that reason is turned into submission and the prevailing conditions are accepted unconditionally. The pattern of one-dimensional thought and behaviour is reinforced by the development of scientific methods in the social sciences. The need for everything to be described in measurable terms results in the empirical treatment of metaphysical concepts such as freedom, equality, and justice, thereby eliminating everything that is spiritual and intangible from people's thinking. The closing of the dimension of critical thought promotes a false consciousness which prevents any real dissociation from the established state of affairs and any real oppositional action.

On the surface modern society appears to be a rational society. It offers a good way of life by providing material goods and apparently satisfying everyone's needs, thus proving that previous societies were inferior. Marcuse, however, contends that it is in fact an irrational society, in which technological developments actually prevent qualitative change, and which alienates its members by restraining the development of their full potential as human beings. Thus, technical progress has resulted in "comfortable, smooth, democratic unfreedom" (Marcuse 1964: 1).

In the political sphere, integration is achieved through a convergence of opposites which negates the power of the working class, thereby subverting the political revolution which Marx foresaw between the working and capitalist classes. This is achieved from two directions. Workers, for example, are offered participation in capitalist enterprises, so that owners and workers strive for the same goals — an increase in the production of material goods. At the same time, the ruling regime, which supports the large organisations, becomes more and more administrative and sublimates the interests of the workers to those of the state. Once again, the satisfaction of material needs ensures that there is no reason to insist on self-determination. The administered life is the comfortable and even the good life (Marcuse 1964: 49).

A similar process of integration takes place in the cultural and communicological spheres of one-dimensional society. The technology of modern mass communications assists the forces of containment by disseminating a pattern of culture determined by the ruling regime. This is a levelling process in which the intellectual and spiritual aspects of human life are controlled and suppressed. Any suggestion of transcending the status quo is thus repelled.

5.3.2.2 Cultural and communicological integration

Marcuse was particularly negative about the American culture industry — the "popular" culture associated with mass production and the mass media — and its implications for the role of traditional "high" culture in society. In pretechnical or two-dimensional societies, high culture was an oppositional culture which embodied the moral, aesthetic and intellectual values of society. Art, music, and literature served to point out the "unhappy consciousness" (Marcuse 1964: 61) or the alienation of people, by pointing out the differences between the actual and the possible conditions of living. Culture could present an alternative way of life because it occupied a position which separated it from everyday living.

Marcuse contends that modern culture is distorted, serving as an affirmation rather than a negation of the established order. Mass production and dissemination make high culture part of mass culture, and in the transformation, it becomes commercialised. The function of pop art, music, films and so on, is to sell material goods, and to comfort or excite its recipients. Art today is a commodity whose cultural values merely serve as instruments of social cohesion. It is unable to invoke a view of reality in contradiction with existing reality because it has lost its aura of separateness. Its critical function has been contained by making it freely available.

Marcuse is not convinced by the argument that mass communication allows culture to reach everybody. Bach as background music in the shopping centre, or Renaissance art in advertisements that sell motorcars, for example, do not serve the function of revealing the contradictions between injustice and freedom, ideology and reality. They merely become part of social reality and integrate images of conditions which should be unacceptable with the conditions of everyday life. Mass art appears to establish cultural equality while covertly preserving domination. The result is that people cannot grasp the contradictions and the alternatives, and the "happy consciousness" (Marcuse 1964: 79) prevails. While people believe that the established system delivers the goods, there is no need for change. Whereas the unhappy consciousness of the past lent itself to political mobilisation, the happy consciousness accepts the contradictions and mitigates against any possibilities of social change.

Marcuse is equally critical of the language of capitalism. He maintains that the possibility of formulating alternative social, political and cultural conditions which qualitatively transcend the existing order is excluded from society by controlling the terminology required to express them. The closed language of modern society is manipulative in that it does not demonstrate or explain — it communicates decision, dictum, and command, leaving no room for protest or refusal. Marcuse (1964: 84) calls this phenomenon "the closing of the universe of discourse".

Marcuse's critique of positivism in the social sciences was mentioned in Section 5.3.2.1 above. By conferring absolute authority on the "given facts", the language of positivism reduces the role and function of thought to the purely passive and receptive task of recognition — that is, of registering that which exists. Concepts such as freedom, equality, peace and justice are metaphysical in the sense that they are not congruent with observed reality. They are thus eliminated from scientific discourse. The result is that positivism gives perception a methodological priority and renders critical thought and alternative ideas redundant.

In addition, Marcuse argues that the conventions of communication that are typically used by the mass media are founded on a faulty or abridged grammar. People become used to the limitations of meanings that such communication provides, the given world is familiarised, and the ability to reason and conceptualise the world in alternative terms is severely inhibited. Examples that Marcuse uses include "a clean bomb" and "harmless fall-out" (1964: 89). He maintains that no language should logically be able to join such opposing terms. The unification of opposites neutralises the impact of "bomb" and "fall-out", and makes discourse immune to the expression of protest and refusal.

In summary, Marcuse's critique of modern man's mode of existence is that he/she lives in a one-dimensional society in which the forces of social, political, cultural and communicological opposition have been contained to create one-dimensional thought and action which renders opposition to existing conditions ineffectual.

5.3.3 Critical assessment

The way in which Marcuse expresses his ideas in One-dimensional man leaves him open to criticism on several counts. For example, his portrayal of American society as totally homogeneous and his pessimistic views about the average person's ability to recognise the conditions of his/her existence, are open to question. The only source of hope that he sees for change comes from "the substratum of the outcasts and outsiders, the exploited and persecuted of other races and other colours, the unemployed and the unemployable" (Marcuse 1964: 256). He seems to overlook the fact that throughout American history, there have been protests about conditions as diverse as racial segregation, abortion laws, nuclear disarmament and the Vietnam war. These protests do not come from the outcasts in society, but from the average citizen. And indeed, after the student demonstrations of the 1960s, Marcuse himself adopted a more optimistic outlook, for his post-1965 writings do not show the same bleak pessimism as One-dimensional man.

Theorists of the left criticise Marcuse (and the Frankfurt School in general) for their view that American society is primarily a cultural system that disseminates false needs, rather than an economic system. While it is valid to suggest that many material needs are created by society and sustained by advertising and economic interests, it is equally true that in socialist countries, the mass media perform the task of promoting the prevailing ideology. It is also difficult to accept that the majority of people, under whichever system they live, will be content with the satisfaction of vital needs only. Human nature seems to drive people towards the attainment of goals over and above what is biologically necessary. That this drive is not commercial in origin is demonstrated by the fact that the leaders in socialist countries are usually provided with far more material luxuries than the man in the street.

Marcuse condemns existing reality in strong terms, but has no positive suggestions as to how it might be changed. It has been suggested that by not aligning themselves with a labour movement, the Frankfurt School failed to provide people with any concrete means with which to translate their theories into practical political activity. Instead, their views were seen as élitist — theoretical, philosophical, and far removed from the reality of everyday living.

However, despite the negative criticism that *One-dimensional man* evoked from both the right and the left, Marcuse's work was not entirely without effect. His ideas on containment were actively pursued by Marxist cultural and media theorists, many of whom tried to provide the empirical evidence that is lacking from his own work. Marcuse's ideas do indeed provide food for thought and an alternative way of looking at society and culture. He was obviously concerned with modern man's mode of existence, and his ideas on containment draw attention to the fact that people in Western societies are not necessarily enjoying a life-style determined by themselves. There is no doubt that the mass media in Western countries help to keep the economy buoyant by promoting consumerism, often at the expense of spiritual values. It is, however, the polemical nature of Marcuse's criticism that is questionable. Raymond Williams (see Section 5.5 below) for example, a cultural theorist who is also concerned with changing the structure of capitalist society, provides a more holistic criticism by showing that cultural ideology is but one of many contributory factors in the shaping of a complex phenomenon such as modern society.

5.4 C. WRIGHT MILLS

5.4.1 Introduction

Charles Wright Mills (1916-1962) is normally regarded as the father of radical or critical sociology in the United States. Like most authors in this monograph, he illustrates the arbitrary boundaries between the (social) sciences. His sociological analysis of "mass" society and its influence on mass communication contributes to a communicological understanding of the complex phenomenon of mass communication in the Western world.

As a loner, Mills was reluctant to align himself with any particular approach. He was influenced by classical thinkers, such as Comte, Durkheim and Weber, but his theory shows greater affinity with neo-Marxism and, in some respects, particularly with the critical theory of the Frankfurt School. The interested reader will find a synopsis of critical theory, including references to the Frankfurt School and to Mills, in Jansen (1989).

Mills is widely known for publications such as *White collar. The American middle classes* (1951), *The power elite* (1956) and *The sociological imagination* (1959). A particularly useful source concerning his ideas is *Power, politics and people. The collected essays of C. Wright Mills*, published posthumously in 1963.

Mills offers a good illustration of the social and cultural approach which was outlined in Section 5.1 above. To elucidate his critique, his point of reference and yardstick for appraising mass society, namely the liberal society, is first discussed, followed by a short outline of important historical changes which shaped contemporary Western society. Finally, some critical comments concerning his communicological contributions are offered.

5.4.2 Mills' critique of mass communication

5.4.2.1 Liberal society and historical changes

Mills' "liberal society" is the American society of the late eighteenth and early nineteenth century, but the structure and mode of existence of this kind of society offer a view of pre-mass society in the Western world. He describes this society as follows (Mills 1963: 187-195).

Pre-mass society had a relatively simple structure consisting of discussion groups or "liberal publics". Continuous interpersonal contact between members guaranteed constant debate and exchange of opinion. Decisions, which were reached through negotiation, were legitimated by genuine public opinion that emerged during discussion. A power balance was thus created and there was no need for a central controlling body to enforce decisions upon subjects. Any mass media which did exist merely extended the free flow of opinions from one public to another.

In the primary public the individual human being occupied a central position (Jansen 1980: 13). Direct, face-to-face contact between participants ensured first-hand experience and understanding, not only of personal circumstances, but of the entire community and of each person's place in it (Mills 1956: 320-322). Thus, in the liberal public, human beings were truly involved and could intervene in events, if and when necessary.

Mills investigates four major historical trends which decisively transformed the liberal society and, by altering the positions of individual participants in communication, produced an entirely different mode of communication as well (Mills 1963: 360-367).

First, bureaucratisation created large structures of executive power in the economic, military and political sectors of society. Since such structures were relatively inaccessible to individual persons, this development severely limited individuals' personal sphere of influence.

Second, centralisation of power was accompanied by intensified attempts at opinion forming. Of great importance in this connection was the rise and use of the mass media by established interests in society.

Third, a new middle class, consisting of white-collar employees who had virtually no access to power, replaced the old middle class of independent entrepreneurs and practitioners.

Finally, the predominantly rural community of publics was replaced by the rising metropolis. Not only did this complex structure allow little opportunity for personal contact; it fragmented people's lives by creating new contexts, each of which only involved part of an individual person's personality. Free flow of opinions was thus disrupted and first-hand experience of events limited.

Mills investigates the new society by examining its constituent parts and their mutual relationships, and studies its decisive influence on the emerging mode of communication, namely mass communication.

5.4.2.2 Mass society and mass communication

Mills' best-known publications concerning this topic are *White collar* (1951) and *The power élite* (1956), supplemented by some of his essays (Mills 1963).

Mass society has a two-part structure consisting of a powerful and a relatively powerless stratum, respectively termed the power élite and the mass. The power élite constitutes the core of the upper classes. It is a ruling minority which wields political power over the entire society. Its members are found in all institutional sectors, but are mainly concentrated in top positions of the political, economic and military institutions. In conjunction with inter-changeable social positions in these sectors, shared interests, personal backgrounds and even similar personality types give the power élite a remarkable unity.

The middle classes constitute the mass, but the middle and lower classes are in fact equally powerless in relation to the ruling minority. Although the power élite's decisions may radically change their lives and circumstances, the ordinary members of society have no means of intervening in their own interest. Due to their position in relation to the power élite, they experience their work as meaningless, they have an underdeveloped political consciousness and constantly experience a status anxiety and a general feeling of insecurity.

Crucial to an understanding of the relationship between the power élite and the mass is the role of the cultural apparatus. This term refers to " . . . all those organisations and *milieux* in which artistic, intellectual and scientific work goes on . . . [and] all the means by which such work is made available to small circles, wider publics, and to the great masses" (Mills 1963: 376). The cultural apparatus is particularly important for the purposes of the present discussion, since Mills regards mass communication as a principal means through which it operates.

The role of the mass media in the relationship between the power élite and the mass becomes apparent in Mills' description of the structure and process of mass communication (Mills 1956: 302-304; 1963: 353-373). Instead of having direct, personal contact, the power élite and the mass only meet through the mass media which address the mass as a mere collection of anonymous individuals, while the communicators remain anonymous as well. The power élite's position in society enables it not only to determine what may be communicated to the mass, but to control all action based on or related to the communicated messages. Any significant influence which recipients may exercise during communication, is virtually eliminated by the fact that the structure of mass communication severely limits their chances to respond immediately and directly to the messages they receive. The power élite is thus enabled to enforce opinions and decisions on the mass.

Mills views the average recipient in mass communication as a passive receptor of whatever message is directed at him/her; the recipient is a mere media market that is continuously exposed to manipulatory messages (Mills 1963: 359). In the final analysis,

Mills considers mass communication as a process of manipulation and control (Jansen 1980: 22).

In conjunction with the other components of the cultural apparatus, the mass media create reality for recipients and control their experience of it. The cultural apparatus is actually the lens through which the mass see the world, a lens which corrects their vision in accordance with standards determined by the power élite who control the cultural apparatus. The mass accept the image of reality presented to them, because the power élite's control over the formation of public opinion enables it to create the impression that it is acting in everybody's best interest.

It should be mentioned in passing that part of Mills' critique of the cultural apparatus is a penetrating analysis of conventional (positivist) social scientific practice which, he claims, serves the interests of the power élite. A brief outline of his criticism may be found in Jansen (1980).

According to Mills the cultural apparatus has three principal existential consequences for recipients. First, since recipients primarily experience events through images created and stereo-types provided by the cultural apparatus, instead of through personal involvement and participation in a genuine exchange of opinion, they become psychologically illiterate. Second, the cultural apparatus provides recipients with a self-image which acts as yardstick for assessing their performance and provides them with an ideal worth striving for. In addition, they are told what to do to achieve the desired result. Finally, the cultural apparatus, particularly the mass media, penetrate into the private lives of people and destroy their privacy.

The overriding existential consequence of the operation of the cultural apparatus may be described as loss of perspective. Constant exposure to stereotyped, limited and deliberately con-strued interpretations of the world deprive human beings of the opportunity to transcend their circumstances and view their lives within the broader social and historical context.

Mills' critique is thus supplemented by a method through which social scientists may help recipients to regain perspective and to engage in interventive action in the interest of meaningful social change. The "sociological imagination" (Mills 1959) is based on assumptions which apply to social scientific practice in general. Mills assumes that the human being is capable of reasoning and of coming to substantiated decisions concerning his/her circumstances. But, given the average recipient's false view of reality, a process of conscientisation is first needed. Mills attributes moral responsibility for debunking the power élite to the social scientist.

The sociological imagination is basically a way of looking at society to find a link between personal problems and public issues (Mills 1963: 395-396). The method, which consists of certain steps, aims at making individuals aware of the structure and historical development of their society so that they may understand their own position in it. In this way Mills hopes to involve the ordinary members of society in a genuine debate concerning alternative viewpoints.

Finally, it should be noted that Mills characterises genuine social scientific practice as intellectual craftsmanship. This craftsmanship refers both to a style of work, which stresses the creative nature of work and its central place in human development as a whole, and to a way of life which accentuates the craftsman's independence, as well as his/her close interplay with a participating public (Mills 1963: 383).

5.4.3 Critical assessment

By showing that mass communication is embedded in the structure of society and that its quality may be significantly influenced by conditions obtaining in society, Mills became one of the first contemporary authors to emphasise the need for critically appraising mass society and its characteristic mode of communication. He has focused attention particularly on the real interests behind the establishment. In addition, Mills contributed to a growing awareness of the possibility that customary social scientific investigation might enhance the perpetuation of the status quo in mass society.

However, by arguing that the structure of society must be changed in order to restore the human being to a creative role in human affairs and in communication, Mills implies that the content and quality of communication are solely determined by the structure of society. This deterministic viewpoint exempts the human being from personal responsibility for the quality of his/her own existence.

A second problem concerning Mills' views stems from his over-accentuation on the significance of political power in society. In his views concerning the liberal society, Mills shows that participants' access to power enables them to achieve a power balance from which the "ideal" characteristics of the liberal society, such as meaningful participation in communication, as well as the mode of communication prevalent in this kind of society, derive. In mass society Mills finds no power balance, a fact which he holds responsible for the problems of mass society. By thus eliminating all other significant factors which may contribute to the make-up and operation of mass society, Mills is forced to present a dark picture of this kind of society and of the quality of mass communication.

Although Mills does not propose a return to the structure of the liberal society, he uses this societal type and its mode of communication as a yardstick in appraising mass society and mass communication. This prevents him from studying mass communication as a phenomenon in its own right and the various mass media as distinctively contemporary modes of cultural expression. And of course Mills does not show how the principles of the liberal society may be embodied in a transformed mass society.

Mills' description of historical changes which shaped mass society and had a significant influence on its mode of existence, contributes to a better understanding of the nature and characteristics of the kind of society in which mass communication takes place. Although authors such as Kierkegaard and Ortega (see Chapter 6, Sections 6.2 and 6.4 respectively) also dealt with this topic, Mills' analysis is more contemporary than theirs. However, when applying Mills' views to contemporary Western society, one should keep in mind that all Western societies are not fully-fledged mass societies and that they do not necessarily share (all) the characteristics of American society either.

Finally, Mills' sociological imagination, which is well substantiated by the views of some foremost Western thinkers, accentuates important principles, such as the social scientist's commitment and the need for intellectual craftsmanship. But Mills fails to show how the steps of his method may be applied to conscientise human beings and mobilise them for action and how the principles underlying this method may be embodied in social scientific practice within a transformed mass society.

5.5 RAYMOND WILLIAMS

5.5.1 Introduction

Raymond Williams (1921-1988) is acknowledged as the most eminent British cultural sociologist of the twentieth century. His ideas helped to transform modern British neo-Marxist understanding of the concepts of "culture" and "society" and their relationship to politics and ideology. The son of a railway signalman, Williams spent his youth in a small Welsh village and acknowledges the influence of closely knit rural community life and working-class values on his thinking. He was a lecturer in drama and literature at Oxford and Cambridge and, at the same time, closely involved in adult and worker education classes. These two different teaching experiences contributed to the way in which his ideas on culture and society were formed.

Williams' many books and articles span a period of thirty years. He was a novelist and a prolific writer on subjects which include literature and drama; social, political and cultural criticism and theory; film, press, television and language. For the purposes of this section of the monograph, it is his views on the relationship between culture, society, mass communication and social institutions that are relevant. These views are found in three early works, *Culture and society* (1958), *The long revolution* (1961), and *Communications* (1962).

As a university student, Williams had been shocked by Oxford and Cambridge's perpetuation of the class system in England by appropriating the British literary tradition as the confirmation of class differences. He became committed to a new conceptualisation of culture which rescues it from élitist and narrow literary and artistic usages. In *Culture and society* (1958) he analyses the work of the major English writers from 1780-1950 to show how the traditional view of culture as a critique of industrial-capitalist society had been taken over in contemporary times as an argument against democracy and socialism. It became imperative to move away from the idea that a minority élite determines cultural taste and to establish culture as "a whole way of life" for all members of society. His intention was to promote a shared and collaborative culture within a socialist community.

✕   *The long revolution* (1961) combines Williams' cultural and political views. He attempts to understand and explain the development of industrial capitalism in relation to the new communication media that were an integral part of it: the press, the popular novel, advertising, and education. He discusses the role of cultural products as ideological instruments and emphasises the social importance of the ownership and control of cultural production and the means of communication.

✕   The subsequent discussion is based on *Communications*, first published in 1962 and reprinted frequently over the years in response to public demand. It is a short but important work which brings together the ideas developed in *Culture and society* and *The long revolution*. His purpose in writing the book was to address what he saw as the problems of British social and cultural policy by describing and analysing the structure and content of existing systems and institutions. He concludes with proposals for social and cultural change which include the reform of the major cultural institutions and the content of popular culture to meet the needs of a democratic (socialist) society.

5.5.2 Williams' critique of mass communication

Underlying Williams' criticism of British capitalist society is his view of the nature of the relationship between a society and its mode of communication. The development of powerful new means of communication in modern times means that there should be a change in the way in which society is defined. Traditionally, society has been described in terms of politics (power and government) and economics (property, production, and trade). Williams (1962: 18) maintains that today "society is (also) a form of communication, through which experience is described, shared, modified, and preserved". He believes that the definition of society and human existence cannot be confined to political and economic contexts. A central and necessary part of social reality is the need to learn, to describe, to understand, and to educate. Thus, "what we call society is not only a network of political and economic arrangements, but also a process of learning and communication" (1962: 19).

   The problem that Williams identifies is that in Britain many people still work from the old definitions of society and regard the growth of modern communications not as the expansion of people's powers to learn and exchange ideas and experiences, but as a new method of government and a new opportunity for trade. All the new forms of communication have been abused, either for political control (e.g. propaganda) or for commercial profit (e.g. advertising). The social institutions are organised to enable the few to govern, communicate with and teach the many. The uses of printing and television, for example, have been shaped by political and economic forces and concomitantly by the imposition of particular communication models which have powerful social effects. Some models, for example, assume that speaking or writing to many people at once is addressing the "masses", or that there are different types of people and interests, and different types of culture. These assumptions have become embodied in the institutions of society. Williams examines the history and content of the mass communication institutions, and the models of communication which they use, in order to find new ways of looking at society and at social relationships.

Williams describes two major factors in the modern history of communications. The first is the enormous expansion of audiences for newspapers, magazines, books, radio, and television. At the same time, even though the extension of communications coincided with the extension of democracy, the ownership of the means of communication has narrowed. Control is in the hands of the sort of financial organisation which resembles the major forms of ownership in industrial production. The methods and attitudes of capitalist business are used in communications with a resulting widespread dependency on advertising money. This leads to the policy of getting a large audience as quickly as possible, to attract and hold advertisers. The old newspaper proprietor, for example, who wanted to control his paper so that he could express opinions is now only interested in how many newspapers he can sell. The basic purpose of communication — the sharing of human experience — has become subordinate to the propagation of a synthetic culture which will sell quickly and bring profits. A concomitant problem is that the same methods that are used by the mass media to market and sell "things" are now used to market and sell people and experiences.

Williams (1962: 91) refutes the platitude that what people buy is what they actually want. He suggests that what is loosely called "culture" in Britain is identified with social and class differences. "High culture" — the work of great artists and thinkers over the ages — is assumed to belong to a particular social minority (the upper classes), while "low" or popular culture is relegated to the majority (the so-called "masses"). Certain interests thus tend to become identified with particular social classes: traditional arts and serious politics for the minority and crime, sex, sport, entertainment and so on, for the majority. The result is a marked division of material into classes. While Williams agrees that there are educational and social differences between people, he maintains that these rigid classifications are not inevitable social facts, but learned communication models which are used to create and reinforce the situation that they describe. They can be altered, but only if traditional British ideas about "the masses" and "classes" change. Identifying "the masses" as stupid and indifferent is a product of history and could be changed, but not while the ruling ideas and control of mass communication remain intact. Williams' (1962: 95-96) way of expressing the inadequacy of current ideas is worth quoting in full.

> First, while we go on talking about 'the masses' we can have neither the respect for people nor the sense of growth that underlie responsibility. Second, while we go on thinking in a separatist way about 'classes' . . . we cannot have sufficiently flexible ideas about people, and will be constantly tempted to divide our culture into separate areas with no bridges between them. Third, while there is an emphasis on profit, there will be a constant pressure to concentrate on things already known and safe . . . [not on] trying new things and offering new ideas and experiences. Fourth, while there is an emphasis on profit and on using the mass communication system as a medium for advertising and selling, there will be a constant pressure to get people into 'the right frame of mind for buying' . . . directing new interests and new opportunities into channels convenient to those with something ready to sell, but not necessarily relevant to the real problems of living itself.

People are thus not getting what they want — they are getting what is imposed on them as a means of maintaining minority control and the profit motive. The reaction of the institutions to any attempts at change is to neutralise and integrate them into a defence of the existing institutions and practices. Williams asserts that this state of affairs exists because, although Britain calls itself a democracy, the communication systems are not free, but are controlled and monopolised by a minority who impose their will on the rest of society. To explain what he means by "controlled" and "free", Williams describes and compares four kinds of communication systems: authoritarian, paternal, commercial, and democratic (1962: 116-123).

In the *authoritarian* system, communications are seen as part of the total machine through which a minority governs a society. The first purpose of communication is to transmit the instructions, ideas, and attitudes of the ruling group. As a matter of policy, alternative instructions, ideas, and attitudes are excluded. In a *paternal* system, the controllers see themselves as guardians, and control is directed towards the development of the majority in ways thought desirable by the minority. Censorship is widely used and defended as being in the public interest. In a *commercial* system, the means of communication is controlled by the minorities with the economic power to market and advertise their goods.

Williams proposes a *democratic* system of control that will result in the mass media being used to create a new kind of culture in a new kind of community — a common culture for an undivided community in which there are no distinctions on the basis of class. A common culture will help to create solidarity among its members. For Williams this is crucial because he believes that before people can exercise personal choice and personal responsibility, they must be made aware of public responsibility and the need to create an educated and participatory democracy.

In a democracy, all people have the right to speak. Thus, the right to transmit and the right to receive is basic and must not be tampered with by minorities. There must therefore be no control by commercial organisations or the state. Theatres and cinemas should be publicly owned; dramatic and film companies, advertising, press, radio, television, publishing, should all be managed by the respective producers, writers and artists. The institutions should be administered by public funds under the control of councils made up of members of society. All decisions to limit communication in any way will be by majority consensus. This will ensure that the role of those who work for the institutions will be that of service to the media and not servility to those in control.

The content of mass communication should be directed at continuous permanent education aimed at the full development of each member of the community and the growth and development of society to its maximum potential. This education should come in the form of programmes on health and family care, adult education, the conservation of the environment, and urban planning to meet the needs of the public for recreation. Education should include the teaching of speech, writing, criticism, and creative expression. (A more detailed account of his proposals for change can be found in Williams 1962: 125-161.)

5.5.3 Critical assessment

Although Williams was committed to social and political change, and his solutions to the problems of modern society thus tend to be reductionist, his concern was above all with the communication process and its place in society. He makes it clear that the system of communication is not secondary, but part of the society to be understood and analysed. His arguments for the extension of communications to provide a "common culture" thus need to be assessed within the context of a class-divided society such as Britain. For Williams, the purpose of a common culture is not to make people alike, but a reaction to the system of meanings and values which a capitalist society had generated, and which was being perpetuated in the social institutions to maintain rigid class differences. His later writings in fact show a deep concern for individual creative expression. Williams' aim in *Communications* is to try to suggest ways of restoring unity to British society by disposing of the "mass" notion and the prevailing élitist view of culture. He saw the mass communication system as the means to bring about a "cultural revolution", comparable in importance to the Industrial Revolution or the struggle for democracy (Williams 1962: 125). Television, for example, is already breaking down class distinctions by extending a minority culture to the majority. It also creates a strong sense of community by providing the means whereby the experiences and values of all members of society can be shared.

The views of society, communication and culture expressed in *Communications* remained the foundation for Williams' later work. His lifelong battle against cultural élitism and his arguments for the importance of the mass media as educational communicators contributed to the formulation of the educational policies of both the Open University and Channel Four, the popular channel of the British Broadcasting Corporation.

Williams was not only concerned with the educational value of the mass media. Much of his later work is devoted to the study of popular culture, which he shows can be a true reflection of society, but under different social arrangements. His work in this field has made a significant contribution to the development of a distinctive British school of media and cultural studies, to the point where today "popular culture" is perceived as *relevant* culture. A comprehensive account of Williams' writings and his contributions to communication studies can be found in O'Connor (1989).

In conclusion, Williams' positive attitude to the place of popular culture and mass communication in society is a refreshing change from the heavy pessimism of many of the writers in this chapter. Compare, for example, his views with those of Marcuse in Section 5.3.2 above.

5.6 JACQUES ELLUL

5.6.1 Introduction

The views of Jacques Ellul (1912-), the French author and sociologist, illustrate a somewhat different perspective on the problems of modern society to those of the other writers in this chapter. Although Ellul criticises Western capitalist societies for eroding democracy with negative consequences for the life of the individual, he does not see a particular type of social system as the cause of the problem. He examines the consequences of having a society dominated by technology and technicians. Ellul proposes that it is the nature of contemporary technological society itself that determines both the power of the social institutions and the inauthentic mode of existence of the individual. He maintains that the organising force in every aspect of contemporary society is a phenomenon which he calls *la technique*. His ideas on this topic are found in *The technological society* (1967), first published in French in 1954. This work represents only one area of Ellul's interests, however. His prolific writings cover a wide range of topics such as politics, law, the arts, education, religion and the mass communication media. They include *Propaganda: the formation of men's attitudes* (1973) and *The technological system* (1980).

5.6.2 Ellul's critique of mass communication

5.6.2.1 La technique

Ellul draws a clear distinction between technique and technology. Technology refers to all the technical practices developed by people since primitive times to serve a practical purpose. Machine technology developed rapidly in Western societies during the Industrial Revolution and was initially directed at the study of techniques that would increase productivity and relieve people from physical labour. The machine thus represents the ideal towards which technique strives. However, the need to increase industry and to develop more sophisticated technological objects resulted in a change from purely qualitative concerns to quantitative concerns. Modern technique no longer concentrates on the development of machinery and its practical applications in industry, but on the development of the rational and efficient methods which today encompass and organise all areas of society — the economy, politics, law, social institutions, and the human being him/herself. It is this qualitative difference in the use of technology that Ellul defines as *la technique*. Technique is no longer the means to a predetermined end; it is an end-in-itself, indifferent to all considerations other than the relentless pursuit of efficiency in every aspect of society.

Ellul is critical of the changes that technique has brought about in the life of the individual. In the past, people controlled the development, use and influence of technology in accordance with human needs and moral values. Today, technique controls people. Its pervasive power has penetrated the whole range of human life so that modern social institutions, for example, are not concerned with evaluating and serving the needs of people, but with the requirements of administrative efficiency — rationality, objectivity, and the use of technological devices. Thus, they do not take into account values such as morality, justice, or even public opinion. Modern society is a bureaucratic society in which the only measure for evaluating the quality of human existence is efficiency.

It is the inherent characteristics of modern technique that accounts for the unbridled onslaught of technology in society. Ellul maintains that in their totality, these characteristics (which are discussed briefly below), combine to deprive the individual of his/her freedom and choice in determining his/her mode of existence. (A more detailed discussion is to be found in Ellul 1967: 79-147.)

Monism as a technical characteristic indicates that in their striving for efficiency, all techniques resemble one another and are inseparably united. The characteristic of technical automation indicates that technology has to find the "one best way" to serve itself. Choice of method, means and organisation is carried out automatically by the technology. People are merely the means for recording the effects and results obtained by the various techniques. In respect of human values, however, technique cannot distinguish between moral and immoral uses of technology. Not only is technique an amoral system, but it creates a different system of values which it imposes on the human being — once it has found the most efficient means, this must be used to capacity. It then becomes immoral to prevent technique from attaining capacity: technology must drive itself to completion.

The spontaneous and rapid growth of la technique is explained by its self-augmenting characteristic. A single American television programme, for example, is carried by several channels, and then expands accumulatively to hundreds of channels across the world by communication satellites, almost without any decisive intervention by people. Universalism as a technical characteristic indicates that the drive for efficiency transcends cultural boundaries and makes all civilisations uniform. In a sense, technique becomes the universal language. Every person in a technological society develops his/her own language peculiar to the area in which he/she specialises, until each person becomes a separate unit, cut off from the rest of his/her culture and from meaningful communication with other people.

To pursue its own course, technique must be a closed, autonomous system, with its own laws for determination, independent of people. In fact, it questions the necessity of people playing a role in the function at all. Technique sees people as the greatest source of error in any system, and thus the greatest cause of inefficiency.

Technique thus attempts to transform people into a more useful instrument so that all its elements can behave as a unified whole.

It is not only the work place that technology has changed, however. Modern technological devices have modified the private aspects of the individual's life — home, leisure, and even his/her conception of time, space and movement. Ellul believes that people feel ill at ease in this new social environment. To perform their tasks efficiently, they must of necessity be made to feel in harmony with their surroundings. For this purpose, la technique creates new human techniques with which to adapt people to its mechanistic requirements. In the process, it suppresses their individuality, emotions, and relationship with themselves and other people.

5.6.2.2 Human techniques and the mass media

The new human techniques are psychological techniques created to adapt the individual's inner life to technical needs, a process which requires the imposition of social and cultural conformity, and the maintenance of a social structure which allows for its unrestrained development. Technological society, in other words, is mass society (see the views of Mills in Section 5.4 above).

The process of massification, in Ellul's view, is not the result of a particular social structure, but the need of mass society to absorb its inhabitants, spiritually and intellectually, into its environment. All the human techniques combine to create a new perception of reality and a new mode of existence. Their ultimate goal is to deprive people of the freedom and responsibility of determining their own lives by suppressing the critical faculty and replacing it with a "good" social conscience; that is, one that coincides with the needs of society. The mass communication media play a decisive role in the process of massification. They perform their most important function in conjunction with the techniques of propaganda (Ellul 1967: 363-375) and amusement (Ellul 1967: 375-382).

Ellul attaches a specific meaning to his use of the term propaganda. Propaganda is not only the dissemination of ideology by individual politicians or mass institutions in order to change public opinion, but a complex of human techniques based on the manipulation of each individual's subconscious to alter the human personality. As a human technique, propaganda has two components. The first is a complex of mechanical techniques (the mass media) which permit direct communication with a large number of people collectively, while simultaneously influencing each individual in the group with its persuasive powers. The second is a complex of psychological techniques which provide exact knowledge of the human psyche. The combination of the two components produces the desired result: the covert adaptation of the masses to technological society through psychological manipulation.

Propaganda not only deprives people of their critical faculty, but causes them to become incapable of choosing between alternatives. They react as the group has been taught to react, irrespective of whether this involves a political decision or the choice of a product. Propaganda is amoral in that the adaptation (massification) of the individual occurs without his/her knowledge or consent. Its effectiveness lies in its ability to act on the subconscious, leaving people with the illusion of choice and free will. Propagandas for particular purposes are developed by sociologists, economists and politicians, for example, and are then popularised by the mass communication media until they are accepted as public opinion. Commercial enterprises such as advertising, film, press, and radio, contain powerful hidden messages which create conditioned reflexes that cause the recipients to buy certain products or think in predetermined ways, until the individual is so absorbed by propaganda that he/she can no longer see the truth.

Whereas propaganda seeks to lead, *amusement* (in the guise of entertainment provided by the mass media) serves to distract. Amusement fills any gaps in the individual's adaptation that might have been overlooked by propaganda. The mass media provide him/her with escape into a fantasy world in which the fears and pressures of everyday life are suppressed. The technique of amusement also fashions his/her interpersonal relationships. People today are not aware of one another as individuals. They rarely engage in meaningful dialogue or have face-to-face encounters. Interpersonal communication is mediated through machines with the result that human relationships have become rational and impersonal. Compensation for subsequent feelings of isolation is achieved by taking refuge in the mass media, particularly in the entertainment provided by television.

Ellul maintains that despite the denial of individuals to the contrary, people in technological society have little choice but to adapt, as they are not able to remain for long at variance with their milieu without becoming anxious and neurotic. In this respect, advertising plays a prominent role. Advertising goes about its massification by first creating a way of life and then influencing the recipient's perception of reality by creating needs which support that way of life. Advertising offers the ideal that we think we have always wanted and turns us into mass people.

In common with Raymond Williams (see Section 5.5 above), Ellul does not place the blame for ideological indoctrination entirely on the mass media. He explains that people's perception of reality is communicated by all social institutions. The mass media combine with education, the law, politics and so on, to keep technological society in equilibrium. Ellul (1967: 348) sees the "new" education, for example, as a social force which utilises human techniques to adjust the child to his/her environment and produce future technicians to serve the state.

5.6.3 Critical assessment

Ellul's major contribution to an understanding of modern society is to show that technology is not an isolated factor in society, but is itself a social phenomenon related to every aspect of people's lives. Ellul's main concern is with the quality of human existence, and by relating technique to the erosion of moral and ethical values in modern life, he places a new perspective on the nature of mass society and the alienation of people from their environment.

Whereas most of the other writers in this chapter tend to overemphasise political and economic power as the cause of the problems in capitalist society, Ellul singles out technology as the central factor in the shaping of society. He is thus prone to reductionism and technological overdeterminism. An important point to take in account, however, is that unlike the technological determinism of McLuhan (see Chapter 2, Section 2.4), Ellul does not regard technology as a neutral force in society. He shows how the control and uses of technology are inextricably linked to the power structure in society, the implications of which extend deeply into social life.

It is not only Ellul's diagnosis of the nature of modern society that is different to that of the other contributions in this chapter. He offers different solutions to the problems as well. He does not believe that a change in social structure will automatically lead to an improvement in the quality of everyday life. People themselves have to first regain control of technology and thereby, the right to choose freely between alternatives; in other words, to live ethically.

Ellul's proposals for change are scattered throughout his writings, and are summarised by Christians (1977). In essence, Ellul proposes that technical solutions to human problems cannot work. The only means of restoring people's spiritual and intellectual life is through "outside" intervention. For Ellul, this takes the form of religion, which he believes is the only way to infuse meaning and fulfilment into modern life. He rejects institutionalised religion, however, and calls for a return to the Judeo-Christian principles of morality and ethics.

Change also requires a transformation in human nature. Only an awakened consciousness can move people away from institutionalised life. To this end, Ellul looks to people themselves, rather than to political ideologies, economic systems, or institutions such as education and government. "I mean the individual who does not lend himself to society's game, who disputes what we accept as self-evident, who finds an autonomous style of life" (Ellul in Christians 1977: 75-76). Such a person utilises internal resources for decision-making and this, for Ellul, is the crux of the matter — only a resuscitation of the private life of people can destroy the tyranny of *la technique* in all areas of society. The awakening of the individual consciousness is the basic requirement for the collective action which will transcend technological determinants in society. In Ellul's vision, the consequences will be "the emergence of social, political, intellectual, or artistic bodies, associations, interest groups — totally independent of technicized forces and thus capable of opposing them" (Christians 1977: 76).

It is arguably Ellul's solutions to the problems of mass society, rather than his diagnosis, that constitute his most interesting contribution to social and cultural criticism.

5.7 SUMMARY

In this chapter the social and cultural approach to a critical appraisal of communication was briefly introduced. Some assumptions of the approach were outlined, followed by a discussion of the views of Orwell, Marcuse, Mills, Williams and Ellul. The authors highlight different aspects of the social and cultural approach and offer insight into its communicological contributions and limitations. The next chapter deals with existentialist critique of communication.

Chapter 6

Existentialist critique of communication

6.1 INTRODUCTION

The kind of existentialist critique discussed in this chapter centres on the emergence and decisive influence of the "mass" in the modern Western world. Generally speaking, "mass" has a quantitative and a qualitative connotation. In modern "mass" society, in contrast to simple rural, pre-industrial society (see, for example, Mills' "liberal society" in Chapter 5, Section 5.4.2.1), large numbers of people are constantly engaged in a variety of activities. However, when reference is made to the quality of their communication, "mass" refers to a particular kind of existence. In the latter case existentialist assessment is almost exclusively negative.

To appreciate their viewpoint it should be borne in mind that existentialists deal with a specific kind of human being that emerged in Western society during the nineteenth century. In their opinion the most significant result of the fundamental social and historical changes of the time was that of levelling. In the place of recognisable individual persons, who were actively involved in society and creatively expressed themselves in communication, a faceless and anonymous type appeared. The "average member of society" can only be described with reference to characteristics shared by all representatives of the type. Hence "mass" stands for mediocrity.

Since existentialists consider communication as a mode of existence which is expressive of the self, they emphasise the need for participants to actively appropriate the meaning of messages to their own circumstances. In mass communication, however, personal appropriation is not invited, since mass media messages

103

address a large audience and tend to follow a standard pattern of presentation. In addition, there is virtually no opportunity for direct feedback. Therefore mass media messages easily operate in a manipulatory way.

Existentialists do not reject mass communication outright, but emphasise the need for making recipients aware of the dangers involved in passively accepting mass media messages. In addition, they suggest principles of communication which may be embodied in mass communication as well.

The existentialist description of the average recipient in mass communication largely concurs with that of the approach discussed in Chapter 5 and both approaches are critical of this state of affairs. However, their different assumptions about society, communication and the significance of (mass) communication for society reflect in their different views concerning the origin of the existential consequences of mass communication and the results they seek in proposed attempts to awaken recipients to an awareness of their condition. For the social and cultural approach the quality of communication is determined by the structure and conditions obtaining in society. Hence adverse effects of mass communication can only be reversed by changing the structure of society through joint interventive action by its members. This approach stresses social solidarity and cooperation for the common good. While not denying the importance of social circumstances, existentialists stress each and every individual person's responsibility for making his/her life meaningful. Since this approach considers self-awareness a prerequisite for awareness of other persons, it stresses the human being's capacity for transcending his/her circumstances in seeking mutually meaningful communication with fellow human beings. Hence, to change the quality of communication requires a change, not in the structure of society, but in the existential choices made by participants themselves.

The remainder of this chapter introduces three well-known existentialist writers, namely Kierkegaard, Buber and Ortega.

6.2 SØREN KIERKEGAARD

6.2.1 Introduction

Since Kierkegaard's views concerning authentic existence constitute the yardstick for his criticism of the daily press as a mass medium, the present discussion must be read in conjunction with

Chapter 2, Section 2.3.2.1. In turn, the outline of historical developments given below provides a context for understanding his views concerning direct and indirect communication in Chapter 2, Section 2.3.2.2.

Kierkegaard lived in turbulent times in European and, more particularly Danish, history. His insight into the nature of the emerging "mass" society, its existential consequences and the opportunities it offered for the development of a new kind of self-expression, is well illustrated by his critical appraisal of the daily press. The scene for the emergence of this first mass medium of the Western world was set by several socio-historical trends of the early nineteenth century, the most important being the following.

First, radical social changes, brought about mainly by the Industrial Revolution, produced an entirely different kind of society. Intimate personal relationships, characteristic of community life at the time, were replaced by impersonal encounters within a variety of institutions where individual human beings now performed different roles.

Second, the first social sciences appeared. Urged by the disruptive consequences of social change, scientists sought solutions for the problems of the time by applying the method of the natural sciences. "Objective" study revealed regularities and patterns of behaviour, but showed no concern for the experiences of *individual* human beings and did not re-establish opportunities for individual involvement and self-expression through communication.

Third, enormous technological development made possible the appearance of mass media, such as the daily press, which radically transformed the customary mode of communication.

Finally, in early nineteenth-century Europe the ideology of democracy and the rise of social movements inspired by the socialist ideal of equality, strongly emphasised that which everybody was supposed to share and distracted the attention from the significance of individuality in human existence.

The joint result of the above trends was a process of levelling which, by producing "the public", replaced individuality with mediocrity. For Kierkegaard it was first and foremost the daily press which created and sustained the public. Hence his critique of the daily press constitutes a penetrating analysis of the existential consequences of the process of levelling.

6.2.2 Kierkegaard's critique of the daily press

In viewing human existence in his day, Kierkegaard observes that everything is becoming homogeneous (Kierkegaard 1970: entry 2061). Human beings are no longer described by their individual characteristics, but by those features they presumably share with other human beings (Kierkegaard 1970: entry 1967). One's "partner" in communication has thus become an anonymous type which denotes everyone and no one in particular. Kierkegaard maintains that the artificial grouping together of people prevents them from having any genuine interpersonal experience of one another. In addition, it prevents individual human beings from becoming personally involved in appropriating the meaning of messages.

This kind of communication is produced by the daily press in particular. The communications of the daily press are directed at "the public" and legitimated by "public opinion", which is created by journalists. For Kierkegaard the public is "a monstrous non-entity" (1978: 91) that outnumbers all people together, but does not represent any single person as such. Since no opinion can be attributed to any recognisable individual person, any opinion or viewpoint can in fact be attributed to "the public" and no one is able to prove or disprove it.

Like the public, the journalist who creates the message, is anonymous. The daily press conveys messages in an impersonal and institutionalised way. The information supplied is said to be "the truth" but, since it cannot be associated with a particular individual communicator, and only the interpretation offered by the daily press and legitimated by public opinion is permitted, no personal appropriation on the part of the recipient is evoked or required and no one in fact determines whether it is "true".

A major consequence of this mode of communication is irresponsibility. When communication does not involve recognisable participants, no one is held responsible for the message or its interpretation. Under such conditions it is relatively easy for the journalist to manipulate the recipient into believing what he/she wants the recipient to believe. It is equally easy for the recipient to

surrender him/herself to the effortless way of life of not appropriating the meaning of messages to his/her circumstances. Lack of
genuine concern and involvement in matters concerning one's life
ultimately leads to alienation. In fact, given Kierkegaard's viewpoint that authentic communication is expressive of the self (see
Chapter 2, Section 2.3.2.1), the creation of "the public" constitutes
a movement towards inauthenticity.

Although an assessment of levelling and anonymity constitutes
the crux of Kierkegaard's critique of the daily press, he refers to
other matters as well. So, for instance, he shows that the contents
of messages conveyed to the public is often of little concern to
people's lives. Yet such messages are presented as if they concern
matters of vital importance to recipients. Combined with a
tendency to unite bits and pieces of information, the daily press is
capable of giving insignificant events a decisive character. The
latter characteristic of "news reportage" is particularly harmful
when it invades the intimate private lives of people and, by creating
impressions on the basis of the construed message, puts misinter-
pretations about them into circulation (Kierkegaard 1970: entries
2156 and 2173).

The ultimate consequence of the communications of the daily
press is mediocrity. The daily press creates the impression that
many, if not all, people think the same way and, instead of
involving him/herself in personal appropriation of the message, the
reader becomes dependent on public opinion created by the daily
press (Kierkegaard 1970: entry 2162).

In *Two ages* Kierkegaard (1978: 70-91 and 102) outlines several
existential consequences of mediocrity. Particularly important are
lack of participation and involvement in communication and in
experiencing events; talkativeness; superficiality and lack of
respect for other people's privacy. In the final analysis, he
maintains, mediocrity reveals emptiness, for it is used as a mask to
conceal lack of self-awareness, awareness of others and self-
expression.

Despite his negative assessment of the daily press, Kierkegaard
does not reject this, or any other, mass medium as such. In fact, he
himself occasionally used the daily press to convey his own
message. To understand his criticism one must consider his
viewpoint that the *way* in which a message is communicated is
crucial in determining its existential significance (see Chapter 2,

Section 2.3.2.2). Thus, depending on how it is used, the daily press may evoke recipients' appropriation or produce mediocrity. Kierkegaard's viewpoint is well illustrated by his attitude towards the satirical newspaper *Corsaren (The Corsair)*.

For Kierkegaard a satirical newspaper is particularly useful for involving the reader in personal appropriation of the message, since the use of irony and satire confronts the reader with opposing alternatives which demand a choice of him/her. In short, a satirical newspaper has great potential as a means of indirect communication (see Chapter 2, Section 2.3.2.2). However, *Corsaren* did not exploit its potentialities and failed as a means of existential communication.

A more detailed discussion of Kierkegaard's critique of the daily press, including *Corsaren*, is given by Jansen (in Perkins 1990).

6.2.3 Critical assessment

The subsequent discussion supplements the critical assessment of Kierkegaard's communicological contributions in Chapter 2, Section 2.3.2.3 by focusing more specifically on his critique of the daily press (mass communication).

Kierkegaard was one of the first and most influential writers who described and assessed the existential significance of the rise of the mass. Especially illuminating in this connection is his account of how mass media, such as the daily press, contribute towards creating "the public" and "public opinion".

Although his investigation concerns the daily press, Kierkegaard offers insight into the social and historical forces which produced and originally shaped the phenomenon of mass communication as such, irrespective of the specific mass media involved. These developments constitute the background to what is today known as "mass communication". Kierkegaard points out that mass communication can never be divorced from its socio-historical context and that it may be significantly influenced by this context. However, for Kierkegaard the contents of human existence is not entirely determined by circumstances. Thus, in the very circumstances surrounding the rise of the mass, he foresaw new possibilities for meaningful individual involvement in communication which, in the final analysis in his opinion, determines the meaning of human existence.

Kierkegaard convincingly shows that mass communication has the potential for not involving recipients in the interpretation of messages, but rather for enforcing opinions and viewpoints on them. This observation is still valid today. In addition, it may seem that Kierkegaard does not accept mass communication as a phenomenon in its own right. However, his negative assessment must not be overestimated. It must be borne in mind that the circumstances of his time made him acutely aware of the potential dangers involved in the new mode of communication and that his only available yardstick for assessing mass communication was the mode of communication prevalent in pre-mass society. Besides, it would be unfair to expect him to have foreseen, at the time of his writing, the full impact of technological and social developments in times to come. In fact, it is precisely his historical position which makes his insight all the more remarkable.

Kierkegaard did not reject mass communication outright. Instead, he was excited at the new possibilities for self-expression offered by this development. Besides, he himself used only mass communication (the medium of the written word) to convey his message and he even experimented with this medium (see Chapter 2, Section 2.3.2.3). A crucial insight on his part is that the existential consequences of communication are determined by the *way* in which the message is communicated, rather than by its contents. Thus the mass media, too, can produce different "results", depending on how they are used, and their potential for involving the recipient should be explored. But it is not entirely clear from Kierkegaard's views how mass media, other than the written word, may be used to involve the recipient in the appropriation of the message. In addition, it is not clear what personal involvement would entail in the case of mass communication.

Kierkegaard emphasises the need for continuous critical appraisal of mass communication. His critique of the daily press points to the danger of all communication becoming "mass" communication, as described by him. And he offers a good illustration of the existential consequences which may follow. However, in contemporary Western society this mode of communication is required to a much greater extent than in Kierkegaard's time. Thus the problem in this unavoidable situation seems to be, not whether mass communication should be used, but how individual human beings may continue to express themselves authentically in modern society and how this can be achieved through mass communication as well. Kierkegaard's contribution lies in his emphasis on the continued need for self-expression, rather than in ideas concerning the form(s) it should take on.

Finally, Kierkegaard's concern with the immense potential influence of anonymous, institutionalised communication points to ethical issues in mass communication and accentuates the responsibility of both communicator and recipient in considering possible negative consequences involved in this mode of communication.

6.3 MARTIN BUBER

6.3.1 Introduction

Buber's criticism of communication and his solution to the problems of modern existence are related to his view of communication relationships. The subsequent discussion should thus be read in conjunction with Chapter 4, Section 4.4.2.2 which deals with his views on dialogue.

Buber addresses and seeks solutions to the problems that people experience in living an authentic mode of existence in contemporary society. He maintains that the history of the world shows that there has been a progressive expansion of the it-world. Each successive era takes on more of its characteristics. In our own time, people live in a predominantly institutionalised world in which they mainly experience I-it relationships and a "seeming" mode of existence (see Chapter 4, Section 4.4.2.2). In the process, true community life and genuine, that is, I-you relationships have disappeared. As the process of self-actualisation takes place between people in dialogue, the individual's potential for living a "being" existence in modern life and becoming an authentic self, is limited. This, for Buber, is the critical issue of modern existence.

At the heart of Buber's criticism is a concern for the restoration of true community in the modern world. He was critical of advanced capitalism because it creates atomised societies in which people cannot live an authentic existence. At the same time, he did not accept the Marxist socialist revolution as a way of creating a true community. He saw it as a system which enforces compulsory

justice and equality. In Buber's view, people must *want* to live in a
changed society. They therefore need to be made aware of the need
to transform themselves and their relationships. For Buber the
crisis of the modern age is thus the question of the individual's
whole existence, not just changes in economic and social systems.
The subsequent discussion of Buber's criticism of modern life and
his alternative proposal — a synthesis of religion and socialism —
is based mainly on the second part of *I and Thou* (1970) and *Paths
in Utopia* (1958).

6.3.2 Buber's critique of communication

In Buber's view, an authentic life requires a balance between the
demands of the you-world and those of the it-world, an oscillation
between "being" and "seeming" in which "being" takes prece-
dence. The problem for people in the modern world is that the
demands of the state and economy have caused them to turn
everything with which they come into contact into objects which
can be put to use. While this is necessary in the world of science
and technology, they have also learned to objectify people, so that
they too are seen as objects of use. At the same time, there is a
corresponding decrease in the power to relate to others. The result
is a deterioration in both the personal (spiritual) life of the
individual and his/her relationships with others (community life).
For Buber, "spirit" does not reside within the individual, but
between "I" and "you" (1970: 89). The individual lives in the spirit
only when he/she is able to enter into relationships with his/her
whole being.

People today have become so reconciled to the it-world that they
do not know how to free themselves and turn to the you-world to
encounter others in relationships. Under these conditions, they
have also forgotten how to reach out to God. The result is that the
individual has divided his/her life with others into two neatly
defined districts which he/she cannot reconcile — the It-district of
institutions and the I-district of feelings (Buber 1970: 92).

Institutions are "out there"; they comprise one's public or social
life, the place where one works, competes, negotiates, administers,
and on so. Feelings are what is "in here"; they comprise one's
personal life, the place where one lives with others and recovers
from institutions. Both institutions and feelings are necessary in

one's public as well as personal life. The problem is that they have become incompatible. The modern state has joined people together without creating or promoting any fellowship between them. There is thus no possibility of true community life.

Merely injecting feelings into institutionalised life is not sufficient. True community is built on a combination of two factors, each dependent on the other. Firstly, its members are all in living reciprocal relationships with one another (I-you relationships). Secondly, the community has a centre towards which all its members are oriented. Buber explains that "the real beginning of a community is when its members have a common relation to the center overriding all other relations . . . And the originality of the center cannot be discerned unless it is discerned as being transpicious to the light of something divine" (1958: 135). Thus, for Buber, the centre is a relationship with God (the I-eternal-You relationship). In his view, one's commitment to God is not manifested in ritual, but in daily living and in relationships with other people. (See Chapter 4, Section 4.4.2.2 for a discussion of the I-eternal-You relationship.)

Buber does not suggest that the it-world is evil or that we should dispense with it. He accepts that people have a necessary desire for success and power, and that not everyone with whom we come into contact can be encountered as "you". What is evil is that the state has taken over to the degree where every trace of a life in which human beings have meaningful relationships has disappeared. The interhuman realm, the "between" where you and I become "we" has disappeared. In the place of dialogue, the prevalent mode of communication between individuals in modern life is what Buber calls false dialogue or monologue disguised as dialogue (1964: 37). In false dialogue the participants do not really have each other in mind, there is no real turning to the other, no real desire to establish mutuality. In situations where people hold different points of view, each sees the other as the embodiment of a falsehood and him/herself as the embodiment of truth. There is thus a widespread insistence on only one point of view and the total rejection of all others.

In this situation, there can be no meeting on the narrow ridge where truth and the meaning of life are discovered (see Chapter 4, Section 4.4.2.2). The individual can affirm neither him/herself as he/she is, nor his/her fellow human being as he/she is. His/her life has progressively become one of existential mistrust: a lack of trust in human existence as such. Buber, however, is convinced that a return to true dialogue is possible. It is not necessary to get rid of institutions, or to deny the needs of the state and economy. It is a matter of reminding people of what they have forgotten — that they have a "you". Once the person recognises his/her you, he/she has the freedom to step out of the it-world and enter the world of relationship. This person is not oppressed by the world of institutions, because he/she can freely move between the two worlds. He/she can oscillate between "being" and "seeming" as the situation requires.

The free person is not bound by fate, but accepts his/her personal responsibility to realise his/her human destiny and create an authentic mode of existence for him/herself. The will to freedom requires a personal decision by the individual. He/she has to choose against the easy course of accepting the dictates of others as well as the temptation to utilise other people as objects for his/her own gain. He/she has to ensure that his/her association with people in the it-world does not inhibit the ability to encounter others in genuine relationships.

The structure of modern society makes meaningful encounters between people difficult. Buber thus suggests that opportunities must be created for people to encounter each other directly. He proposes a socialistic restructuring of society in the form of a decentralised state of smaller and larger communities, which exist over and above the structures of society. People in such communities voluntarily choose to live and work together and thereby create a meaningful life for themselves. This does not entail a levelling process, but a genuine living together of people who are aware of their differences, but also of their common responsibility. Buber believes that the best example of community life is to be found in the village communes (*kibbutzim*) established by the Jewish immigrants in Israel. Although the commune could be improved in many respects, Buber calls it "an experiment in cooperative or community living which did not fail" (1958: 139). It did not fail because it was not enforced, but grew out of the immediate needs of people who built their community around a common centre.

In such a community an authentic mode of existence is possible because the we-relationship is actualised. The we-relationship begins as a dialogue between I and you, but it can be extended to include several people who relate directly with one another. Buber (1964: 213) explains as follows: "By We I mean a community of several independent persons, who have reached a self and self-responsibility .... The We includes the Thou potentially. Only men who are capable of truly saying Thou to one another can truely say We with one another."

Buber's ultimate intention was the establishment of a community of communities within the state, each relating dialogically to the others. The eventual outcome would be a world federation of nations which, like the individual communities, would be linked through the principle of dialogue.

6.3.3 Critical assessment

To gain a complete picture of Buber's contribution to the study of communication, the following discussion should be read in conjunction with the assessment of his theory in Chapter 4, Section 4.4.2.3.

Buber's views provide insights into the problems of modern life and the role of communication in causing as well as overcoming some of the problems. He was not the first existential theorist to relate the problem of contemporary existence to the deteriorating relationships between people. However, having died in 1965, Buber was able to situate his arguments more explicitly within the specific circumstances of the contemporary situation than, for example, Kierkegaard or even Ortega (see Chapter 6, Sections 6.2 and 6.4 respectively).

Buber contributes to our understanding of the role of communication as a mode of existence in the modern world in several ways, of which his concepts of the between and the we-relationship, and his views on community life are the most relevant. In seeking a solution to contemporary existential problems, he looks beyond the individual and the structure of society to a third alternative — the relationship that is formed between people in dialogue. Buber emphasises the central role of the between in both the personal and social life of the individual, and the necessity for people to transform themselves and their relationships to improve the quality of their lives.

Although Buber did not address the problem of mass communication directly, his analysis of I-it relationships describes the type of communication that we associate with the mass media. While he did not provide a particular method to solve the problems of mass communication, his concept of "we" makes a contribution to an understanding of the problems. By extending the idea of dialogue to include more than two people, he suggests that it is possible to overcome some of the problems associated with mass communication, such as the impersonality of the message and the persuasive motives of the communicator — provided that the participants themselves make the effort to overcome the limitations.

Buber's idea of a socialistic restructuring of society has both advantages and limitations. While the type of communes that he envisages provide ideal circumstances for direct relationships, Buber himself acknowledges that they can succeed only under specific conditions. He criticises the Soviet socialist regime, for example, as a forced system of community living that does not provide the spontaneity required for meaningful relationships. The idea of a commonwealth of communities across national boundaries linked through the principle of dialogue is also open to question. Buber's own attempts to establish a bi-national state in Israel failed because he could not get Arabs and Jews to negotiate a joint settlement for developing the land. It would seem that when political issues are the subject of discussion, the participants are more concerned with their vested interests than in trying to establish the conditions for dialogue.

Arguably, Buber's most important contribution lies in the application of his views on community to the existing conditions of modern life. Arnett (1986), for example, suggests that Buber's ideas could assist groups and organisations in becoming human communities, rather than places of association. They could in fact contribute to improving relationships in all situations where people live or work closely together, and where polarised communication (false dialogue) is often taken for granted — in one's family, circle of friends, school, business and professional life. Ultimately, however, the decision to create reciprocal relationships, for example, to listen attentively to others, respect alternative points of view, reveal one's inner self, and affirm others as the selves that they are, remains the choice and responsibility of each individual.

This point of view clearly shows Buber's existentialist emphasis (see Section 6.1 above).

6.4 JOSÉ ORTEGA y GASSET

6.4.1 Introduction

The Spanish philosopher, José Ortega y Gasset (1883-1955), is well-known for his critical appraisal of human existence in "mass" society. His views constitute a variety of the extentialist position outlined in Section 6.1 above. Apart from *The revolt of the masses* (1969), first published in 1930, his publications include *The modern theme* (1961), first published in 1923, *Man and crisis* (1959), first published in 1933, and *Man and people* (1957), first published in 1934.

Events in Spain, as well as Ortega's personal background, exerted a powerful influence on his views, the purpose of his writing and the solutions he sought for the crisis of his country. His parents were well-known figures in journalistic and literary circles in Madrid and his family controlled the leading liberal newspaper in the city. Thus he was introduced to the world of critical debate and cultural production from a relatively young age.

1900   At the turn of the century Spain experienced disillusionment and disorientation, brought about by modernity and aggravated by political problems and widespread poverty. A growing spirit of individualism interfered with national unity. An important event was the fall of Spain as a mighty colonial power in the New World. Socio-political change of the time radically transformed the major institutional sectors of the country. Although disillusioned young intellectuals, known as "the generation of 1898", were actively involved in a renewal of literature, science and philosophy, they failed to moderate the anarchy which was caused by the upheavals of the time. Events inevitably culminated in the Spanish Civil War (1936-1939) which was, in turn, a prelude to the Second World War. A detailed account of the Spanish scene is provided by Wohl (1979).

Ortega, who was convinced that an intellectual minority should educate the masses, set himself the task of making his countrymen aware of the crisis and uniting them in the national interest. Publication was his vehicle for this purpose.

The subsequent outline of Ortega's critique of mass man is introduced by a short description of his views concerning individual human life and the generation, which act as yardstick in his critical appraisal. The discussion concludes with an assessment of his communicological contribution.

6.4.2 Ortega's critique of the masses

6.4.2.1 *Individual human life and the generation*

Human life is first and foremost individual life or, as Ortega puts it, individual human life is "radical reality". "Radical" does not bear the connotation of superior or only reality; it refers to the fact that all other realities appear and exist in the individual person's life. Not only is human life personal; it is untransferable. It is the life of each person and no one is capable of experiencing events on someone else's behalf (Ortega 1957: 39; 58).

An important implication of this viewpoint is that a person becomes aware of life only when he/she becomes aware of him/herself, and life is meaningful for the human being only in as far as he/she experiences it. Ortega adopts the phenomenological viewpoint (see Chapter 4, Section 4.3.1) that the human being is capable of distancing him/herself from the world in order to come to terms with him/herself through contemplation. Having thus discovered him/herself, the human being returns to the world to act in it (Ortega 1957: 16-18).

Action takes place within one's circumstances, a concept which refers for Ortega to everything which surrounds the human being in the physical and social world. "To live" actually means to be constantly engaged in establishing, through interpretation, a meaningful relationship with one's circumstances (Jansen 1975: 12).

However, what a person regards as the meaning of his/her life derives largely from those collective interpretations which are passed on from generation to generation and constitute "reality". The most important kind of collective interpretation is *creencias* or absolute beliefs which are held by society and thus remain in force irrespective of a particular person's acceptance or rejection (Jansen 1975: 12-13). As such, *creencias* constitute the principal form of life at a given time, the "spirit of the times". Although *creencias* enable the individual human being to structure his/her otherwise chaotic surroundings in order to establish a relationship with his/her circumstances, they do not entirely determine the contents of human life. *Creencias* are never perfectly integrated; hence doubt arises and the human being is forced to seek, through contemplation, solutions to the problems thus created.

In seeking to establish a relationship with his/her circumstances and to solve life's problems, the individual human being adopts various perspectives. Ortega's perspectivistic viewpoint culminates in his concept of the generation which is particularly relevant to the present discussion, since a distorted communication relationship between the members of co-existing generations is for Ortega indicative of the revolt of the masses.

In explaining the generation, Ortega starts from the viewpoint that human beings are differently placed vis-à-vis their circumstances and, consequently, that all human beings do not approach the same socio-historical circumstances from the same viewpoint. Different perspectives are ultimately determined by differences in age.

For Ortega age is the fact of finding oneself in a particular sector of one's limited lifespan and of looking at the world from a particular viewpoint. Thus, age is not merely a chronological fact, but primarily a way of life (Jansen 1975: 11). Persons of the same age constitute a generation and are in turn young, mature and old together. Contemporaries of different ages represent different generations. A generation may be distinguished from other co-existing generations by its peculiar set of perspectives, which is expressed in cultural productions, such as the arts and sciences. Thus Ortega maintains that each generation has its own distinctive "vital style" (Jansen 1975: 15-17).

As each generation passes through the chain of generations, its perspectives are reconsidered and renewed in order to keep its members in living contact with their ever-changing circumstances. As long as human beings interpret their experiences meaningfully, human life is dynamic and ever-evolving.

However, the members of the generation are not equally creative and capable of producing guiding perspectives. For Ortega the generation consists of two components, namely the élite or select minority and the mass. It must be emphasised that Ortega's élite is not distinguished from the mass by access to and/or abuse of political power. He adopts an aristocratic view; the élite is an intellectual or cultural minority that is constantly involved in creating culture. And culture in fact refers to the totality of solutions to life's problems available to human beings in a particular society at a given time.

The élite is distinguished by a life of effort, achievement and excellence in the cultural field, while the mass is inert and passive (Jansen 1975: 20-21). Ortega concurs with the existentialist view of the mass as being an anonymous type of person, that is, everyone and no one in particular (see Section 6.1 above). The élite, in turn, comes close to his description of authentic human life, since it seeks loneliness to contemplate the meaning of its circumstances and returns to the world to act according to the perspectives thus constituted.

Ortega describes the relationship between the élite and the mass as one of "dynamic compromise". By interpreting their circumstances, as well as the typical experiences of the mass, the élite provides the mass with a framework of guiding perspectives for approaching life's problems. Perspectives are not enforced on the mass; they only become operative through the consent of the mass.

The élite-mass relationship described above depicts the "normal" relationship among the members of the generation. In contrast, "mass man" signifies a distorted relationship in which the mass rejects the élite and communication between them breaks down completely. This phenomenon involves all co-existing generations of a given time and therefore reveals the quality of existence in an entire society. In fact, Ortega maintains that the revolt of the masses is characteristic of the entire Western world.

6.4.2.2 Mass man or the revolt of the masses

The mass's rejection of the élite ultimately signifies the rejection of the guiding perspectives provided by the élite. Without perspectives, which apply specifically to its circumstances, the mass has no means of determining the meaning of circumstances for its life. Stranded with an alien set of perspectives, created by previous generations, it is deprived of vital contact with its world. In The revolt of the masses (1969) Ortega investigates the ensuing "historical crisis".

Ortega finds the main reason for the rejection of the élite in the existence of a strong cultural system. The mass which is inherently passive is tempted to accept what is available, rather than to try to assess the élite's proposed framework of perspectives. The inevitable result is that culture becomes saturated and stagnant, while the mass becomes increasingly more "cultivated" and self-alienated.

Ortega maintains that some historical changes of the late nineteenth and early twentieth century enhanced the development of "mass man". For instance, technological development produced a world of superabundance. Human beings now enjoy privileges without having made any effort to create the world which offers them the privileges. Democracy, in turn, promises people equal rights on the basis of presumed equality. In addition, it appeals to all members of society to subscribe to the average and to align themselves with those who presumably share their circumstances. The joint result of these trends is that life becomes increasingly more collective and less personal. In short, mediocrity rules the day.

Although no individual person may be distinguished in the mass, it is no longer anonymous. "Mass" now signifies a type of human being that rejects individuality, asserts his/her rights everywhere and tolerates no opposition, but enforces his/her will, even by means of coercion. Political leaders, for example, deny their subjects opportunities for participating in decisions concerning courses of action and appeal to "public opinion", which they themselves create, to legitimate their actions.

Lack of guiding perspectives ultimately results in uncertainty and instability. The mass lives in confusion, debasement and bewilderment, its inner emptiness forcing it to join the ranks of whoever promises security (Jansen 1975: 30-31).

Although the historical crisis described above may last for centuries, Ortega does not equate it with decay. Crisis eventually leads to the downfall of the masses and forces them to subject themselves to a new élite. Under such circumstances a decisive generation appears to bring about fundamental change and renewal in the prevailing mode of existence (Walgrave 1967: 110-111).

6.4.3 Critical assessment

Ortega's analysis of the revolt of the masses offers insight into the socio-historical forces responsible for the rise of the mass and highlights some defining characteristics of this human type. His description of the nature and characteristics of its mode of existence is particularly valuable, since it shows the decisive role of a distorted communication relationship in producing its "revolt" and determining the existential consequences thereof. Although his analysis concurs in many respects with that of Kierkegaard, he highlights the existential consequences of levelling within a more contemporary context.

It should be noted that Spain, first and foremost, was Ortega's point of reference. Although the gist of his interpretation is applicable to Western society, he was undoubtedly influenced by conditions in his own country. The influence is perhaps most evident in his exaggeration of the negative existential consequences of the rise of the mass and in his uncritical acceptance of an aristocratic view of society. In the latter case Ortega's position tends towards élitism, as he does not provide for independent and fully-fledged cultural production on the part of the mass. But it should also be noted that his concept of élite does not restrict membership and participation to the higher social classes, or to any other dominating group, and that he maintains that the élite in fact expresses that which is inherent in the mass. In fact, the élite only exists by virtue of the mass.

Ortega does not explicitly refer to mass communication but, by stressing the active involvement of the mass in determining the suitability of the élite's proposed perspectives, he captures that kind of relationship which existentialists would like to see embodied in mass communication. However, he does not clearly outline the process of compromise between the élite and the mass; nor does he show how the élite may set about to guide the mass. However, in his description of the revolt of the masses, he illustrates the consequences of one-way communication in which "recipients" refuse to participate in a meaningful exchange of ideas with the "communicator".

Since the revolt of the masses arises from stagnation of culture, Ortega sounds a warning that repetition of the same format and/or content in mass media messages may produce messages of inferior quality and that this state of affairs may contribute to uncritical acceptance, instead of personal appropriation of meaning, by recipients. Ortega forcefully illustrates how mediocrity may choke an entire society.

Finally, he suggests that the content of human existence is not entirely determined by circumstances, but that it is determined rather by those perspectives which attribute, or fail to attribute, meaning to the possibilities and limitations offered by circumstances. In short, he confirms the phenomenological argument concerning the human being's capacity for creating a "life-world" of meaning over and above his/her circumstances (see Chapter 4, Section 4.3.1).

6.5 SUMMARY

In this chapter existentialist critique concerning the quality or condition of the phenomenon of communication was introduced. Some assumptions of the approach were outlined, while the greater part of the chapter was devoted to the critique of three well-known writers, namely Kierkegaard, Buber and Ortega y Gasset. The critical assessment of their respective contributions offers insight into the value and shortcomings of existentialist critique of communication in general.

Résumé

This monograph is offered as an introduction to general communication theory. In the first chapter some misunderstanding concerning the nature of theory and its shaping influence in the entire process of scientific investigation was clarified. Following from the viewpoint that theory is basically a body of theoretical approaches, an attempt was made to delimit the field of general communication theory.

In the remainder of the monograph some of the major theoretical approaches in this field were explored. Each approach was defined with reference to its assumptions concerning communication and a representative theory was discussed and critically assessed to illustrate the approach and its communicological value.

Theoretical approaches discussed in the monograph offer a multi-dimensional view of communication and accentuate the fact that any single approach inevitably presents a limited interpretation of the phenomenon.

This inherent limitation emphasises the need to know the merits and shortcomings of available approaches to be able to determine their suitability for investigating particular aspects of communication. Likewise, it emphasises the need for better understanding and cooperation between researchers and theorists in promoting the growth of the discipline of Communication Science.

Finally, the theoretical approaches discussed suggest differences of opinion about several aspects in the field of theory. An ongoing debate and critical appraisal of the usefulness of theoretical approaches are vital to the growth of any scientific discipline. It is therefore hoped that this monograph will stimulate a fruitful exchange of ideas.

SOURCES

Allen, R.C. (ed.) 1987. *Channels of discourse: television and contemporary criticism*. London: Methuen.

Arnett, R.C. 1986. *Communication and community*. Carbondale & Edwardsville: Southern Illinois University Press.

Barthes, R. 1967. *Elements of semiology*. London: Jonathan Cape.

Barthes, R. 1972. *Mythologies*. London: Jonathan Cape.

Bennett, T. 1977. The Frankfurt School and the critique of the "culture industry", in *The study of culture*. Milton Keynes, London: Open University.

Buber, M. 1958. *Paths in utopia*. Boston: Beacon Press.

Buber, M. 1964. *Between man and man*. London: Collins.

Buber, M. 1965. *The knowledge of man*. London: Allen & Unwin.

Buber, M. 1970. *I and Thou*. Edinburgh: Clark.

Christians, C.G. 1977. Jacques Ellul's concern with the amorality of contemporary communications, in *Communications*, Vol.3 No.1:62-80.

De Fleur, M.L. & Ball-Rokeach, S. 1975. *Theories of mass communication*. Third edition. New York: David Mckay.

Ellul, J. 1967. *The technological society*. New York: Vintage.

Ellul, J. 1973. *Propaganda: the formation of men's attitudes*. New York: Vintage.

Ellul, J. 1980. *The technological system*. New York: Continuum.

Fauconnier, G. 1985. *Aspects of the theory of communication*. Cape Town: Academica.

Fiske, J. 1985. *Introduction to communication studies*. London: Methuen.

Friedman, M. 1976. *Martin Buber. The life of dialogue*. Third edition. Chicago: University of Chicago Press.

Gadamer, H-G. 1977. *Philosophical hermeneutics*. Berkeley: University of California Press.

Gadamer, H-G. 1985. *Truth and method*. London: Sheed & Ward.

Goffman, E. 1975. *The presentation of self in everyday life*. Harmondsworth, Middlesex: Penguin.

Hawkes, T. 1986. *Structuralism and semiotics*. London: Methuen.

Heidegger, M. 1967. *Being and time*. Oxford: Blackwell.

How, A.R. 1980. Dialogue as productive limitation in social theory: the Habermas-Gadamer debate, in *Journal of the British society of phenomenology*, Vol.II No.2:131-143.

Jansen, N. 1975. *Generation theory*. Johannesburg: McGraw-Hill.

Jansen, N. 1980. *C. Wright Mills: social critic*. Cape Town: Academica.

Jansen, N. 1985. Martin Buber: die lewe as dialoog, in *Communicatio*, Vol.II No.1:35-44.

Jansen, N. 1986. Søren Kierkegaard: haltes op die lewenspad, in *Communicatio*, Vol.12 No.2:2-8.

Jansen, N. 1989. *Philosophy of mass communication research*. Cape Town: Juta.

Jansen, N. 1990. Enkele gedagtes oor die rol van teorie in die wetenskapsbeoefening, in *Communicatio*, Vol.16 No.2:14-18.

Jefferson, A. & Robey, D. (eds.) 1985. *Modern literary theory*. London: Batsford Academic and Educational.

124

Johannesen, R.L. 1971. The emerging concept of communication as dialogue, in *Quarterly Journal of Communication*, Vol.62 No.4:373-382.

Kierkegaard, S. 1962. *The point of view for my work as an author.* New York: Harper & Row.

Kierkegaard, S. 1967. *Søren Kierkegaard's journals and papers*, Vol.1. Bloomington: Indiana University Press.

Kierkegaard, S. 1970. *Søren Kierkegaard's journals and papers*, Vol.2. Bloomington: Indiana University Press.

Kierkegaard, S. 1978. *Two Ages*. Princeton: Princeton University Press.

Littlejohn, S.W. 1983. *Theories of human communication.* Second edition. Belmont, California: Wadsworth.

Lowrie, W. 1942. *A short life of Kierkegaard.* Princeton: Princeton University Press.

MacIntyre, A. 1970. *Marcuse.* London: Fontana/Collins.

Marcuse, H. 1955. *Reason and revolution.* London: Routledge & Kegan Paul.

Marcuse, H. 1956. *Eros and civilization.* London: Routledge & Kegan Paul.

Marcuse, H. 1964. *One-dimensional man.* Boston: Beacon Press.

McLuhan, M. 1962. *The Gutenberg galaxy: the making of typographic man.* London: Routledge & Kegan Paul.

McLuhan, M. 1974. *Understanding media: the extensions of man.* London: Abacus.

McLuhan, M. & Fiore, Q. 1967. *The medium is the massage.* Harmondsworth, Middlesex: Penguin.

McQuail, D. 1975. *Communication.* London: Longman.

McQuail, D. & Windahl, S. 1981. *Communication models for the study of mass communications.* London: Longman.

Mills, C. Wright 1951. *White collar. The American middle classes.* New York: Oxford University Press.

Mills, C. Wright 1956. *The power élite.* New York: Oxford University Press.

Mills, C. Wright 1959. *The sociological imagination.* New York: Oxford University Press.

Mills, C. Wright 1963. *Power, politics and people. The collected essays of C. Wright Mills.* New York: Oxford University Press.

O'Connor, A. 1989. *Raymond Williams: writing, culture, politics.* Oxford: Basil Blackwell.

Ortega y Gasset, J. 1957. *Man and people.* New York: Norton.

Ortega y Gasset, J. 1959. *Man and crisis.* London: Allen & Unwin.

Ortega y Gasset, J. 1961. *The modern theme.* New York: Harper & Row.

Ortega y Gasset, J. 1969. *The revolt of the masses.* London: Unwin.

Orwell, G. 1979. *The collected essays, journalism and letters of George Orwell*, Vol.1. Harmondsworth, Middlesex: Penguin.

Orwell, G. 1980. *The collected essays, journalism and letters of George Orwell*, Vol.2. Harmondsworth, Middlesex: Penguin.

Orwell, G. 1983. *Animal Farm.* Harmondsworth, Middlesex: Penguin.

Orwell, G. 1984. *Nineteen eighty-four.* Harmondsworth, Middlesex: Penguin.

Palmer, R.E. 1982. *Hermeneutics: interpretation theory in Schleiermacher, Dilthey, Heidegger, Gadamer.* Evanston: Northwestern University Press.

Peirce, C.S. 1931-58. *Collected papers.* Cambridge, Massachusetts: Harvard University Press.

Perkins, R.L. 1990. *International Kierkegaard commentary: the Corsair affair.* Macon: Mercer University Press.

Saussure, F. de 1974. *Course in general linguistics.* London: Fontana.

Schutz, A. 1962. *Collected papers*, Vol.1. The Hague: Martinus Nijhoff.

Schutz, A. 1967. *The phenomenology of the social world.* Evanston, Illinois: Northwestern University Press.

126

Schutz, A. 1970. *On phenomenology and social relations*. Chicago: University of Chicago Press.

Schutz, A. 1976. *Collected papers*, Vol.2. The Hague: Martinus Nijhoff.

Stearn, G.E. (ed.) 1968. *McLuhan: hot and cool*. Harmondsworth, Middlesex: Penguin.

Steinberg, S. 1989. *Dramatic dialogue: an approach to an understanding of interpersonal communication*. M.A. dissertation. Pretoria: University of South Africa.

Walgrave, J.H. 1967. *De wijsbegeerte van Ortega y Gasset*. Utrecht: Aula.

Williams, R. 1958. *Culture and society*. Harmondsworth, Middlesex: Penguin.

Williams, R. 1961. *The long revolution*. Harmondsworth, Middlesex: Penguin.

Williams, R. 1962. *Communications*. Harmondsworth, Middlesex: Penguin.

Wohl, R. 1979. *The generation of 1914*. Cambridge, Massachusetts: Harvard University Press.

Young, P. 1988. Ellul on technological forecasting, in *Futures*, April 1988:194-197.